Rod.

With love
& best wishes.

Caroline
& John -

* July '98

A BREATH FROM ELSEWHERE

A BREATH FROM ELSEWHERE

Musings on Gardens

MIRABEL OSLER

BLOOMSBURY

First published in Great Britain 1997
Bloomsbury Publishing Plc, 38 Soho Square, London W1V 5DF

Copyright © 1997 by Mirabel Osler

The moral right of the author has been asserted

A CIP catalogue record for this book is available from the British Library

ISBN 0 7475 3037 8

10 9 8 7 6 5 4 3 2 1

Typeset by Palimpsest Book Production Limited,
Polmont, Stirlingshire
Printed by Clays Ltd, St Ives plc

CONTENTS

Introduction
1

I
*There Are No Right Ways to Make a Garden –
Only Alternatives*
5

II
The Germination of a Garden
56

III
Surfing the Flower Beds
88

IV
Growing to Love the Plants I Hate
146

V
Dead-Heading the Guilt
175

*Some of the Books, People and Places
Referred to in the Text*
215

Index
216

For Michael

'I wept, as I remembered, how often you and I
Had tired the sun with talking and sent him
down the sky.'

A BREATH FROM ELSEWHERE

Musings on Gardens

Introduction

This book grew out of a chance remark made to me by a librarian. She spoke of the sad sight of elderly people browsing among the gardening shelves on wet afternoons, desperately looking for answers to the question of how to cope now that they were the sole owners of gardens they had inherited.

The comment, vivid and too near for comfort, gave me the inspiration for the book. A sort of alpha–omega of gardening. It begins with people who have never gardened before and who, though tempted, are still hesitant, and continues with others who have already launched themselves into the unknown region but have not yet found their bearings. The last chapter is for those at the end of their gardening lives: for widows and widowers, partners and lovers, who may be struggling to keep the garden going but who can't release themselves from it without being overwhelmed by guilt.

A BREATH FROM ELSEWHERE

The title, *A Breath from Elsewhere,* is intended to make it quite clear that the book is diametrically at odds with practical gardening books dealing with classic or formal gardens, small, winter, container and scented gardens, *et al.* These are full of photographs, sound advice, expertise and useful facts. Here are neither pictures nor know-how.

There are no photographs, because most gardening books with pictures are not physically readable. They can't be held comfortably to be read on a train, in bed or in the garden. They need to be propped up by a couple of bricks on a table. I do read books like these sometimes, but supporting them on the dining table isn't exactly what I relish at nightfall. I know that garden inspiration can be gained from page after page of coloured photographs, especially when one is inexperienced and searching for incitement, but they undervalue the written word. No one reads the text in these books, only the captions. Soon we'll be able to identify an author by reading a caption.

My first chapters may sound naïvely unsophisticated to gardeners who have gone way beyond them, but they are drawn from my own experience of starting a garden. I can recall the force with which uncertainties were thrown up amid all the felicity.

My knowledge of gardening is meagre, yet however often I reiterate this boring fact, people won't believe me. Sometimes I'm asked to design a garden, but to do that you need your wits about you. First catch your wits; mine deserted me years ago. I can't remember names – either of people or plants – but because I write books that are rooted in gardens, people think I know what I'm talking about. But I don't. Any advice I give is subjective. I write only from limited experience, gained from making one garden with my husband in the country, and one on my own in a town. That's all. But these two undertakings have led me all over the place, through labyrinthine conjectures to chasing after plant collectors, flowers in art, textiles, tiles, poetry and God knows what else – but never, absolutely never, towards the cold frame or into a propagating shed. The loss is mine, but that's the way it happened. Gardens took me on in a manner over which I had no control. I can give no foolproof solutions, but I can tell you what worked and what didn't in these two gardens, and hope, by passing on my successes and failures, that some bits may be applicable to you.

More and more people are making gardens. I don't know who counts them, but annually the figures are rising, which must say something about the human spirit. And it isn't just the obvious people – the competitive or the discontented; the middle-aged, the retired or separated; the thwarted painter or the frustrated genius. Many new gardeners are young. They are people with jobs, small children or part-time work; people who live in cities or who are commuters. They are the thousands who need breathing space and a place for creative licence all their own. Often leading hectic lives, they yet make time for this other dimension that is unique, personal and financially unremunerative.

It seems lamentable that, despite this interest in gardens percolating through to younger and younger people, children aren't given more exposure to the world of plants. Children react with uncluttered spontaneity; they can look,

touch, breathe and smell flowers with none of the preconceptions and cerebral assessments that beset us. The
intricacy of a plant seen through a magnifying glass has
as dynamic an effect on a child's imagination as reading
about Alice's discovery of a bottle labelled 'Drink Me'.
Children are still young enough to be confounded. Yet
how many have a chance to feel the woolly leaves of
'Lamb's tongue' (*Stachys lanata*), or to discover through
touch that a poppy's scarlet petal feels as fine as silk
between their fingers? A child's wonder is instantaneous
on finding that what look like prickly stems on a robinia are
really as soft as the velvet on the antlers of young stags.

Certain flower scents imbibed when one is young are
fixed unconsciously and indelibly in the psyche. Years later
a smell of primroses, hawthorn, lilac or a certain rose may
resurrect instant childhood. And if children aren't put off
by being asked to do garden chores there's a good chance
that they'll want a little piece of ground for themselves, or
else that at some much later time in their lives they'll find
those early memories have germinated, and the filaments
of nostalgia have become as strong as tap roots.

CHAPTER I

There Are No Right Ways to Make a Garden – Only Alternatives

Gardens are refuges. In search of replenishment we retreat to them as to a safe haven. They have none of the threatening attributes to be found in more dramatic escapes: lone voyages, wilderness, deserts – or drugs. There is no need to pit your endurance against the elements, to feel challenged or to prove yourself to yourself. Gardens act as a solace and a panacea. With their innumerable qualities we use them in a variety of ways, for inspiration or freedom, for discovery or surrender.

Whether our responses are botanical or visionary, a garden works without the menace of intimidation. By using all five senses we retrieve areas of ourselves that may have been ossified far too long. Outside, tending a garden, an unsought restitution takes place. Considering how we are daily besieged through mass communication by horrors in life that stab us in the heart or the back,

then planting a lily may miraculously be all that's needed
to bring us upright again. But why, and how? Why do
gardens restore a sense of equilibrium in so many ways?
What fermentation or elixir of invisible salubrity lurks in
the earth, that doesn't exist in the swimming pool, on an
historic tour, up a mountain, or between the sheets? Gardens are unique. And under stress at any age, gardening
is far more efficacious than running 'worry' beads through
your fingers or taking to the bottle.

Garden Visiting

Practical books are the gardener's Baedeker. Their dead-
pan information may be invaluable but they have done
nothing to nourish my excesses. At the start, a different
sort of book did that: those with misty photographs, of
colour in foreign places; pictures where I could recognize
flowers or plantings so hideous they cleared my head of any
ideas in that direction. But no book, in whatever category,
emphasizes the benefit to be gained from visiting gardens,
an essential pastime. By merely looking, osmosis occurs
and almost subliminally one starts to make judgements.
The diversity of gardens can be as overwhelming as it is
helpful. Yet visiting must be done – at least it must by those
of us who are devoid of self-confidence as well as plant
expertise. And the more a garden reflects the owner's temperament and taste, the more interesting visiting becomes,
activating the uninitiated to sort out their own foibles. But

goodness, gardens are hell. Once you begin they push themselves, with all their pulsating alternatives, into the forefront of your thoughts until, too readily, you become a predator clutching at every idea.

Visiting gardens can be a contentious subject. There are some who say that when they first started they didn't want to be influenced by other gardeners and other gardens; that could come later. Because their plans had been gestating for so many years, when the opportunity did finally come they chose to start with a mind uncluttered by extraneous promptings. This method is direct; what is in the mind is so visual that no sketchy or confusing outlines are needed. Michael, my husband, and I were not this sort. We thrashed about from the outset. We had to visit an arboretum to see what a tree looked like. We went to long-established gardens to see what had gone on before, and we returned often to watch the progress of gardens in the making by people who knew what they were about. We required to know what plants did what. We looked, we noted the relationship between plants and structure; and long before autumn, before the planting season, we went to a nursery to see roses at their summit of flowering. We left feeling even more callow and confused. There were so many quite beautiful roses that we became hopelessly acquisitive. If we had known, it might have been better to have had some sort of rational shopping list, limiting and modest.

But ideas can be hoarded, though they may be inappropriate at that particular moment. We made notes anyway. One I filed away was the sight of a small island in the centre of a pool on which bulbs had been so densely planted that at a certain time of the year the island looked like a vessel floating up to its gunwales from the weight of tulips. Another time, while I was walking somewhere, I slowly became aware of trickling water. It was so hidden that it took time to locate. What mattered was the audibility, not the vision. Other things noted in our book were the sight of six-foot-tall crambes diffusing the gaudiness of flowers planted behind them; *Lilium regale* rising from a shaggy ground-cover of decorative ivies; the improbable sight of *Holodiscus discolor* cascading over an orange wall; and espaliered fruit trees forming an irregular barrier to peonies and asparagus growing behind them. The list of things seen in other gardens was endless. It didn't matter that the impeccable topiary in some places depended on a fleet of gardeners to maintain it: we noted it anyway. Everything can be reduced in scale and adapted and used for your own particular effect.

For six or seven months of the year our heads were filled with stimulation, envy, provocation, irritation, disappointment or delight. And though I wanted to look through my own eyes, I also wanted to look through the gardeners' eyes. It's not just that I may admire what I see; I seek the immense pleasure of talking to the owners themselves, even though I may be running to keep up with their erudition. A garden doesn't float detached from the person who created it. There are two languages to be translated: that of how the place speaks to you, and later how the gardener speaks of the garden. We may have ended as ignorant as when we started out, but I used to feel on returning home that my head was pulsating with images of things I couldn't live without.

Looking at gardens is beneficial at any time, but particularly when you begin and particularly if, as we were, you're lucky enough to have near you somewhere in the making that's open to the public. A little ignorant ogling does wonders. You can watch development over the months and years, learning from someone else's labour, errors and successes. Not far from us is Stone House Cottage Garden, belonging to Louisa and James Arbuthnott, begun in the late 1970s and gaining momentum during the 1980s. It was possible to watch it and the nursery flourishing with what seemed to us prodigious speed. There we could witness the growth rate of yew hedging, of wall plants and of trees, and at the same time occasionally have our hands held when we were in crisis over some disaster or other and needed calming advice.

Years ago Michael and I visited another well-known garden near us. We were surprised on that first visit to find broad flower beds with deserts of weed-free earth between the plants. The garden is new, we thought. Next year it'll be different, the earth won't show. We were wrong. The gardener wanted it like that; he liked the orderliness, the isolation of one plant from another, the neat and controlled appearance with nothing allowed to overhang the razor-sharp edges of a pristine lawn kept in tip-top order. Even sixteen years on, weedless earth still creates an antiseptic illusion of immaturity. It also flattens the spirit: no one could come away from there dancing.

Then there are gardeners whose places are crammed to bursting as they push in more and more plants they swear they cannot live without. The effect is extravagant and throws out such a sense of reckless generosity that you leave the garden feeling a nicer person than you really are. Yet I know others who have looked at something – a viburnum, perhaps – and said 'Oh I'd love one of those, but I've nowhere to put it!' Nowhere to put it? But I've seen the garden! It's one vast lawn with a few shrubs and trees dotted about and some narrow beds of stingy dimensions. Don't argue, though, hold your tongue. People who have no sense of profligacy sing in a different key; arguing produces only discord. Anyway, as we all have our hang-ups surely it's diplomatic not to offer an opinion when it hasn't been asked for? Yet I love it when someone visits my garden and makes a dogmatic statement: 'I'd have that out if I were you!' – or, more sinisterly: 'It looks fine for now.' Being taken aback by something done months ago that hasn't been in the forefront of my mind ever since is salutary, and at times inspirational. How easy it is to become familiar with things and to forget to look with a fresh assessment. When a friend suggests raising an urn off the ground or moving a seat to a different site, or tells me to stake the yews with an iron rod if I want them to grow straight, I like it. What's more, I really do appreciate that people have bothered to look constructively at what they see. Often their comments lead to verbal pyrotechnics, from which comes some completely extraneous idea neither of us had foreseen.

Vicarious gardening should not be underestimated. Observing how hedging changes a design or how colours coalesce or how long it takes a pool to become choked are prime lessons that sort out your own priorities.

* * *

What do you look for when you visit a garden? We each have a pre-set bias. We approach a garden with antici-pation to find – what? Plants? Flowers that are bizarre and exotic? Ingenuity of design both practical and fulfil-ling? Or, arriving vacant, do we need to shred apart the ingredients, to analyse and then copy at home someone else's comely planting? Some of us hope to receive a small piece of inspiration, like a precious fragment, to be handled at our leisure; some are on the look-out for ideas, for form and for hard facts to be tucked into mental pockets for later use. Others are tentative, approaching a new garden without preconceptions but with mind and eyes wide open, hoping to be filled by the sagacity of another whose sense of grandeur, aplomb and general stylish achievement bowls us over with their vitality. And for some of us there may even be a mild form of prurient curiosity as we find, disclosed by the look of the garden, hidden recesses of another's personality – the bit that, until now, has been kept well out of sight. For without doubt, looking at a garden is a form of undressing the owner's ego.

To be taken over or taken in, or to surrender?

As far as I'm concerned, when visiting a garden I'm not on the look-out. My mind is disorderly, unstructured, and I don't need to know – or only later: I need to feel. My ideal is to drift unquestioningly, lured onwards by what is just through the next opening, at the end of the path or across the bridge. It has nothing to do with intellect, with cerebral mastery or the naming of plants. The convenience of Latin passes me by. What I want on first entering a garden is submersion: to be sapped of identity, to look through narrowed eyes and, with luck, to end overwhelmed. That would be my perfect outcome. But thank goodness we're not all as hopeless as that. Some of the friends with whom I go visiting gardens appear to hold their intelligence in their hands on the threshold. They hold it out like a divining rod, something jutting out ahead of them as antennae on an insect do. Their enquiring minds gather learning by the handful, slotting it away with intellectual avidity. Fortunately we are different. Gardening would have got nowhere if they'd all been like me. My garden appreciation rides on the backs of all those people – starting with the plant collectors – who do have their wits about them and who do know what they are seeing. Quivering with curiosity, they are continually pushing out the frontiers of horticultural knowledge. Unlike me, they aren't just wading about in a vacuous sea of ignorance, hoping to be astonished.

Gapers and Crouchers

Garden visitors divide into two sorts: the Gapers and the Crouchers. Each sees a garden differently. The former throw back their heads, sniff the air and open up their sensual vents, while continually altering their focus. They come to bask, and to leave rekindled. The Crouchers, on the other hand, progress through a garden (theirs or someone else's) with tunnel vision and a permanent stoop. When finally they leave the premises they have in their hands a list of accurately-named plants – their booty – to be followed up at home with a search in the invaluable Royal Horticultural Society's *Plant Finder* for nurseries to supply each plant. But what they miss! They enter a garden with knees bent, specs on, and never, not for one moment, do they walk erect, take deep breaths, sense the atmosphere, assess the prevailing mood, absorb the overall quality, or respond to its impulse. Competitive and acquisitive, they move blindfold along paths, never 'seeing' the garden, merely flexing their botanical muscles.

I sigh when a Croucher comes here. It doesn't happen often because my garden is a dead loss, it's not a place of rare delights. But my buoyancy goes limp, particularly when they say threateningly: 'Can I come and see what you've got that I haven't?' ('Not a thing, not a thing,' I murmur as an aside.) Inevitably he or she is going to leave here disappointed. The first thing they do is to start dropping names, the Latin ones, to prove to me that they know their onions. But it's wasted on me. I wouldn't even know if they are right or wrong, but I do know that I'm to be quizzed on 'Which one?', 'Surely not?', 'Can you really grow this here?' (A winter's bark, *Drimys winteri.* No, the answer is, I can't. It died last summer.) They move along the path doing what I call the Vincent Square shuffle. This needs an explanation. Vincent Square is where the Royal Horticultural Shows take place. They are oases of wonder in the heart of London and they draw devotees from far and wide. Their seasonal exhibitions are places of floral virtuosity; here we can pause with myopic stance and not be thought batty. Plants are on display that you would die for. Instead of having a watering mouth – as I do when standing in front of market stalls in France – my eyes water, from boundless admiration and a hopeless longing doomed to be unrequited. Oh, to have such unbelievably beautiful works of floral art in the garden. To have such peerless blossoms; to have one such ravishing plant from among this throng. I defy anyone to leave Vincent Square not walking on air. Trails of us return homewards enveloped in an aura of scent and colour, and with a sweetness in our souls that wasn't there when we left.

When Crouchers come here and dampen my spirit by performing the Vincent Square shuffle, I know for certain that we are two different sorts of gardener, each seeing the place through subjective eyes; they'll leave here not having picked up the quintessence of what I'm struggling to achieve. On an autumn day recently, a Croucher walked through the garden so intent on the ground that she never noticed her reflection in my mirrors, progressing at the same pace alongside her. 'No dahlias!' she cried in dismay. Well – no, actually, though it hadn't occurred to me. Since then, having seen her garden, I understand. Her garden was exploding with dahlias and begonias. She'd come hoping to find in mine unsuspected treasures that she hadn't known about. People like this return home unaware of my attitude to the whole complexity of gardening; unable even to see what has worked for me and what hasn't. Far too intent on the lexicon for their personal 'plant finder', they restrain their chagrin and never come here again.

We are so out of kilter that I become downcast and feel more and more protective towards my garden; the visitor is condemning it as a failure and I'm overcome by a kind of Prince Charles plant empathy bordering on lunacy. 'There, there,' I say. 'I love you.' Even so, I've many friends among the Crouchers, and all the time I'm writing this I know that we desperately need and rely on them. They are genuine Plants People; they are as vital to our gardens as rain, because it's through them that the variety of our gardens has grown.

So with a certain remorse for what I've just written, I do make a mental genuflection to the Crouchers and Great Collectors. After all, it was Captain Francis Winter – one of Drake's men – who in 1575 was responsible for the discovery of my deceased and much-lamented *Drimys winteri*.

These two ways of looking at a garden – the Crouchers and the Gapers – were made most apparent to me when, on a humid and stifling day in August, I visited a friend's town garden, jammed with spectacular trees underplanted with spring bulbs but then, in midsummer, verdant with ferns. Ferns of every sort, rare and outlandish, sculptured and fretted, were growing from well-watered leaf mould. As the gardener named each one in a continuous litany, while he progressed doubled up, I was able to follow his bottom, free to absorb the jungly illusion of the tree canopy overhead and the transforming quality of the green luminosity. The dappling of light, the steaming poultice underfoot and the tropical atmosphere clinging to my skin held me enthralled. Latin names? The minute variety of scrolling leaves, identified by my friend one after the other, had no power over me. I was imagining gaudy butterflies and red-whiskered bulbuls glimpsed through the clammy foliage. It was an experience I shall never forget, but I rather think my host imagined that I left with a totally different imprint.

Crouchers move through a garden at a stoop: naming, gasping, hooraying, admiring or coveting plants; Gapers saunter, smiling or sighing at what they find, succumbing to an intangible beatitude that takes them for a brief escape into another dimension. Both sorts of gardener are besotted; both get their hands dirty, think and talk gardening; but on the threshold of another's garden, each uses a different set of whiskers.

The Third Eye

There is a third category of visitor, not to be underestimated. Their views (I really mean views, not opinions) of our gardens are invaluable. They are the photographers.

I'm intrigued by them and by the way their eyes work. I have been, ever since the first professional came to our garden in the country. Photographers use their eyes quite differently from the rest of us. If we could exchange them – if for an afternoon I took mine out and lent them to a professional photographer while I borrowed hers or his – would I come any nearer to understanding their way of looking? I believe that what a photographer sees in a garden is at variance with how a writer sees it. When I write articles for magazines in which the visual look of gardens is the star of the show, and the whole production depends entirely on the photographer, my role is to see things with a part of me that has little to do with eyes. Of course looking at the garden matters, yes; responding to atmosphere and sensing the spirit of place have nothing to do with the technique of looking, but all to do with unseen appraisal – with feeling, and even with gut. I want to be moved. I want my skin to get goose-pimples and the hair on my neck to stand up, at something which no camera can catch. Seeing gardens through my own eyes at the same time as being impelled to see them through the delicacy of a lens is like fiddling with the focus on my binoculars.

Photographers observe what I don't; their eyes are organs I don't possess. What are they seeing that I can't? What are they looking for? Whatever it is, photographers are constrained by the margins of a frame. My eyes, though they may be focused on something definite, take in a whole lot of blurred imagery at the sides, where colours appear in a diffused haze, in undefined shapes and out-of-perspective impressions. But they, the photographers, are narrowing their retinas to an exact point. The way light works is decisive and where lines merge is paramount. Foreground, background, verticals and horizontals for them take on an absolute status. Their eyes are devices tuned to operate with the precision of a laser. But are they telling the truth? Or are they deceivers, adept at concealing what lies just beyond the perimeter? Does a photograph reveal the 'thatness' of a garden? Is a photographer putting in our hands irrefutable evidence or a piece of artistic reflection – subjective and louche – proof, merely, of the photographer's singularity? They raise our sights. On the visual level, naturally, but also by tempting us to reach far further than our capabilities. If what they show us is so peerless that everything we're looking at seems hopelessly unobtainable, we may not risk even starting. It's all very well to sigh and get carried away by the photographer's art if you happen to be a welder or a banker and your spare time is spent on the golf course or at the races – anywhere but in a garden – why not keep turning the pages? But if you have tentative aspirations to make a garden, one glance at some of these photographs may send you into turmoil just as easily as it enthrals you. Photographers are consummate sorcerers.

When I look at a perfect combination of plants trapped forever in a photograph I despair, knowing that I shall never achieve such visual integration. But then I take comfort from wondering what was just outside the frame. Some scrappy, over-leggy daisies? Sagging abutilons, or woody lavender smothered in buttercups? That's how life is, really. There's always some bit of random intrusion I haven't got under control.

Watch these people at work. I like the way they move with feline caution round the garden lugging gangling-legged objects and strings of impedimenta as they survey this or that quarry. Sometimes, unimpeded by gear, they prowl, stalking their prey with single-minded intent. Watch how a photographer holds a gadget to the light. Almost in supplication he or she offers it skywards to the deity of optics. That done, they splay the legs of a tripod in unlikely places; fiddle with apertures; stoop and peer intently, and even then may not be satisfied. Moving the gear fraction-ally to left or right they concentrate, minutely observing . . . what? They pause, screw up their eyes, step forward, step back, performing a solitary dance having left their partner abandoned, with legs straddled, waiting to be taken back into a familiar and protracted embrace. I'm bewildered too by how profligate professional photographers are with film. They may take as many as twenty shots of a single view. Or so it seems to me.

A prisoner in my house, I keep looking from the window, trying to see what they see. I note the clouds, the shadows, a sunny glitter or impending storm, and yet I remain bewildered. I envy their intensity. Nothing distracts them from the alliance between the eye and the lens. It's with difficulty I stop myself from tapping on the window and calling softly: '*Now* what are you staring at? Five minutes you've been stuck there.'

When photographers come to this garden – and it isn't a large place, only a long town enclosure – I know that I must allow them their freedom. I'll have prepared for their arrival in advance by clearing up strewn leaves on the paving, sweeping back bits of escaped gravel, tying up a strand of jasmine to hide a bare length on the ceanothus; I'll have given the rosemary, lavender and box a hair trim and then meticulously gathered up the bits (something I'm usually sluttish about). Even so, somewhere I've overlooked a few fallen petals; my unseeing eye has passed them over as part of the garden, but the photographer borrows a dustpan and brush to sweep up the few strays that, shamefully, I hadn't even noticed. And it's not only outside that needs a critical eye. Photographers don't want washing-up liquid, tins of cat food or an empty Château-Latour bottle (chance would be a fine thing) standing on the kitchen sill. The picture of honeysuckle draped around the window must not be flawed by mundane objects of little artistic merit. Then there's the weather: regardless of the wind, the cold, or whatever is inclement that day, they need to leave the back door ajar for a look into the half-revealed hall. I hear the wind whistling along the passage, the door behind me slamming shut as, stuck in front of the word processor, I stop to put on yet another pair of socks.

A metal café chair, painted the yellow of the rose 'Maigold' against which it stands, is so tempting to one photographer that he moves it about the garden as if I've furnished the place with two dozen of them. Another thing: when a professional is photographing my garden (and I do appreciate it's her or his livelihood and time is of the essence) I can't step outside for a moment without letting out a warning call. How mortifying to stick my head out at the very moment a great shot is being taken.

Please Alex, Andrew, Georges, Ianthe, Jerry, Jill, Marianne, Phillipe and Vyvian – don't think I don't love you. I do, I do. I'm just overcome with envy that I don't possess your patience. I have tried. I even bought my own camera two years ago, when I took a group of Americans on a fortnight's tour based on a book I've written on French gardens. It was no good. As soon as I walked into a garden holding this compact device made for simpletons to my eye, I couldn't bear it. As far as I was concerned, I was paralysed; with one eye shut I would try to home in on something I thought I ought to photograph, but all the time I was missing 'seeing' the garden. How could I limit my view to an 'autofocus window' and a 'snap-shooting button'? I found the procedure distracting. When I'm in a garden I want to saunter, to pause inert as a sponge absorbing what surrounds me. I want to linger in archways, push open a door in a wall, be seduced by paths with no end and, if it's there, to succumb finally to a sombre verdancy of trees.

A camera, even one so user-friendly as to have an exposure sensor, has for me no place in this appraisal. So from Avignon to Normandy, and ending with some gardens in Paris, I never used my camera. I had neither the patience nor the heart. But I was the only one on that tour who didn't. From one side of France to the other, all my group spread like flocks of birds about the handsome grounds of the gardens we visited, indefatigably taking snaps. It seemed to me that far too seldom did they spare a moment to look with both eyes open. With one eye welded to the viewfinder, did they see the subtle shapes in a garden without flowers in the Lubéron; reflections of trees in a dark pool in Provence; the variations of light among thickets of roses in a garden on the slopes of Lyon; or the subtle pastel shades of grasses among herbs in Normandy? Weeks later I thought of them, in Oregon and Virginia, Boston and New York, looking at their photographs. Did they sometimes stop, trying to recall which garden was which; and did they pause to wonder what it was that had been just out of sight of the frame?

When I look at the photographs of this garden taken by professionals, I'm nonplussed by their discerning eyes. I'm also flabbergasted. Can those pictures have been taken here? Is that beautiful, sensitive, unbelievably ravishing paradise *this* place? My garden? What's happened to the wheelbarrow? The telephone wires? The pile of frost-shattered pots, the rose not yet dead-headed, the self-seeded scarlet poppies and the inextricable tangle of clematis? And where's the puce Judas tree and the psychedelic cherry in a neighbouring garden? Bamboozled, I realize that these photographers have seen visions that entirely passed me by.

Few gardens have perfect pitch; but with a photographer's sleight-of-hand they can be made to appear miraculously harmonious.

Only beautiful people worry about how they look in photographs. The rest of us faced reality long ago. Looking at our own images, we expect nothing. If we appear better than we thought we did, we can bob the head in gratitude towards the photographer's skill. If we look worse, it isn't a shock; we'd expected nothing else. But beautiful people have so much to lose. This was brought home to me recently when a friend insisted that I should tear up a photograph I had of her talking beside another friend in her garden. 'I look pregnant,' she protested. 'You must destroy it!' I hadn't even noticed, neither her stance nor the flow of her dress. Her looks are so stunning no one would ever notice her waist, and I just liked the picture of two of my friends standing in a pretty garden. But she wouldn't have it. Reluctantly, as she was obviously so upset, I allowed her to tear the picture to bits – bits too small to be retrieved and stuck together when her back was turned.

As I walked home I thought how frail, how near the surface and vulnerable is self-regard. Another beautiful friend who has made a beautiful garden is just the same, and will never allow herself to be photographed. She daren't risk it; yet both garden and woman enhance each other. She and I do a lot of far-flung jaunts together, visiting places before the school holidays begin and she goes under. We enjoy it so much – partly because she is a professional, which means that we look with different eyes. Yet on the way home we nearly always agree as to whether we'd return to that particular garden again.

Someone else with whom I often go garden visiting with shared enjoyment and conclusions on what we've seen – whether derogatory or rapturous – has quite different demands from mine. She has an insatiable appetite for noting down every single plant that is disease-free and will stay in flower for months on end. 'Remontant' on anything ensures that it is put into the boot of the car. Everything she plants in her garden must come almost with a guarantee of a phenomenal flowering span. She demands immortality from her plants; well, almost – protracted life, at least. That's an aspect low on my priorities when I go to a nursery. I'm looking for other attributes: if a plant pleases me, the brevity of its life is immaterial.

The result of these differing criteria is that her garden is colourful from early in the year and without drawing breath till late autumn, while mine moves in bursts and pauses, and by winter the absence of colour is barely noticeable.

A final word to my friends who are gardeners. Certain ones are so self-effacing that when I visit them they assume I want to see their gardens – not them. I'm not allowed a brief whisk round the beds before we sit down together for the bit of tittle-tattle which is what I've come for; instead, I'm force-marched from plant to plant, pausing frequently to be told this is in the wrong place, and what has been afflicting those others.

But they couldn't be more misguided. It's them I've come to see! It's my friends I care about, it's his or her life, in the wrong or right place, that concerns me – not the plant's. I want to share whatever might be afflicting their souls, not their alstroemerias. By all means let's sit in the garden; but for me our conversation, *tête-à-tête*, and the relaxed communion of friendship far outweigh the blow-by-blow account of every plant and its history up to the moment it ended here. Please don't underestimate yourself, dear friend. I've come for our shared warmth, for verbal intercourse, for trivial gossip and the affectionate reassurance of being with an intimate crony.

A single-minded fixation on gardens is to me as tedious as mothers who go on about their infants, those who continually bring the conversation back to their cats, or men so hooked on cars they can't pass one without kicking the tyres. Yes, I know their defence: if I were a real friend I should accept that the garden is the biggest thing in their lives. And unfortunately, because I write about gardens it's presumed they are in mine too. But they aren't. Oh God, they aren't! By autumn I've had enough. I've had it up to here. It's time to extend the horizon. Months of bending, looking, gasping, admiring, discussing, buying and planting have left my garden-attention span at nil. There are so many other things in the world I have never seen or done; so many other things to talk about, films to see, galleries to visit, books to read. And above all, I long for laughter. It's one of the great relaxers in life and I can't get enough. Laughing bounds through the body convulsing every part: not only is the mind in a state of high delirium, but the lungs contract and expand with unexpected flexibility, arms are clenched as the agony of laughter doubles us over, and tears run down our cheeks. And afterwards? After laughter, oh, what state of total relaxation. A sense as of thawing takes over our muscles, they become fluid, and we gently return to normality, picking up from where we started. Tell me, how often do gardens do that for you? No one can honestly say they are places that generate hilarity.

So by autumn I don't want to talk about gardens; I want to look beyond the corymb and umbel.

Gardeners Who Push Out the Frontiers

Some people have pushed out the parameters of garden innovation to fabulous limits. These are the gardeners who break boundaries. In the Lubéron in France is Nicole de Vésian, who has made a garden without flowers for the sake of seeing shorn blue-grey 'boulders' of santolina, lavender and sage harmonizing with the Provençal landscape surrounding her. The garden is sculptured, calm, and as full of carefully-sited stones as it is of shrubs.

Sylvia Breakwell, another friend who refuses to conform with what is acceptable and not acceptable in the horticultural landscape, bought an abandoned piano for two pounds and put it in her garden because, as she told me, 'I love what the piano is made of': wood and ivory. The fact that left outside it would decay along with fallen petals and cabbage stalks was irrelevant. She wanted to enjoy its slow disintegration through the seasons, to witness tall grasses thrusting up among the strings. 'I just loved the idea of a musical instrument being taken over by nature,' she explained. 'Well, it's all back to nature, isn't it?' Next to her piano is a slightly chipped peppermint-green Art Deco wash-basin. In summer Sylvia fills the basin with ice cubes and champagne bottles while a tape stuffed down the innards of the instrument produces ghostly sounds of Winifred Atwell playing piano-roll music. 'I don't want tranquillity in the garden,' she said. 'I'm more interested in being challenged.' At present she's surrounding the piano with a hedge of contorted willows. 'You see, I love contortion!' In another part of the garden she's making a Japanese dry river-bed – 'Gardens should be sculptural.' And then, turning to another favourite subject – a total *non sequitur* – she spoke of rabbits. Describing the garden she was making for them, she said: 'I don't want the rabbits in cages, I like them moving about.' Her husband was fashioning their rabbit house and 'there'll be drainpipes for them to run through, and railings snaking round outside.' I could see it all; she was right, it was challenging. It certainly prodded one out of apathy. Thank goodness for deviancy, for a lack of conformity, and for a sense of fun.

Private gardens where the impetus comes from abstraction and the use of artefacts are at the other end of the range from those created out of sculptured wilderness. At Grizedale in Cumbria is a forest where any time of day or night the public can wander freely among

Andy Goldsworthy's sculptures: dead trees as massive as cathedrals, pillars of stone, and vegetal debris that has been turned into woodland creatures on a framework of wire, moss and bracken.

At opposite ends of Britain are two other archetypal gardens. One is at Dungeness, on the remote southern tip of Kent. On a piece of flat land at times swept by salt-laden easterlies, and at others concealed by mists is the late Derek Jarman's fisherman's cottage. In the distance, under a vast sky, is the brooding presence of a nuclear power station. Jarman evolved the garden out of anything that surrounded him: driftwood, shells and cork floats, stone circles, iron sculptures and rusty detritus. Planted among shingle are the survivors, the plants that withstand a climate of relentless extremes: poppies, thrift, comfrey and cabbages; gorse, salvias, chicory, cistus and many others of a fleshy endurance or spiky durability. '. . . so many weeds are spectacular flowers: the white campion, mallow, rest-harrow and scabious look wonderful,' Jarman wrote. 'Introducing these local flowers into the garden makes a little wilderness at the heart of paradise.'

Derek Jarman didn't compromise; he accepted what was there. Others might have gone to war, feeling challenged to pit themselves against such a ruthless terrain. They would have built walls, fences or shelter belts (as Osgood MacKenzie did on his peninsula at Inverewe on the western coast of Scotland) to deflect the sea wind in an effort to coerce plants sighing for the solace of the Cotswolds. The strength of Jarman's garden lies in his integrity; he stayed with what attracted him in the first place, rather than manipulating the landscape into something else. His legacy is a unique garden without boundaries, either to itself or of the spirit.

At the other end of Britain, nine hundred feet up a hill in Lanarkshire in the south-east Highlands, are seven acres of wilderness. The land belongs to G.F. Dutton, a scientist, poet and wild-water swimmer who for forty years has worked within this piece of marginal land. To tussle with nature when there are early and late frosts, short and rainless summers and arctic winters when snow lies across the land for eighty days may sound like folly, and only someone with imagination and a pronounced tilt would maintain such an ongoing confrontation. Nothing is benign; surrounded by antagonism, Dutton has created a dramatic theatre from the trees, boulders, torrents, gorges and moorland. Continually fighting invasive and vigorous encroaching vegetation, Dutton has with care chosen those plants and trees that could withstand the onslaught. Flowers are not top of the list. Yet in spite of climatic hostility, and by working with, not against, the native flora, he has coerced and manhandled his land into cloisters, each with its own character. Across turf, heather and mossy floors, through glens and gorges, are planes of greenery and arches of foliage sculptured into receding vistas.

Like Derek Jarman in Kent, Dutton, acknowledging what is indigenous, has created his garden accordingly. Determined that '. . . the picture will not clash with the splendidly muscular stride of landscape . . .', his attitude is one that many British gardeners living abroad would do well to adopt instead of crucifying themselves in their attempts to recreate 'English' gardens, lawns and bosky groves in a desiccated landscape and an extreme climate under a molten sky. Rather they should heed the wisdom of Derek Jarman and G.F. Dutton, whose 'gardens' expand the boundaries by their mixture of ingenuity and acquiescence.

Both these gardens were made by using what surrounded them. From a quite different impetus is the cerebral garden of Ian Hamilton Finlay at Little Sparta in Lanarkshire. His place is idiosyncratic, deviant, provoking, and certainly rum. Quizzical inscriptions appear on trees, stones and sundials, unsettling visitors by transporting them onto another plane. Amid four and a half acres in which sculpture, artefacts, flowers and thistles appear to be self-sown, Finlay's garden moves through facets of the spirit. People who have been there come away enchanted, but the beauty and enigma of Little Sparta remain with them long after they have come down to earth.

As I repudiate with heartfelt conviction the assumption that there are any right ways to garden, I resent how the media try to brainwash us into thinking there are certain acceptable designs and incontrovertible rules guaranteeing a perfect end result, while all else is unacceptable. If you ever need proof of how wrong they are, visit Ivan Hicks's garden. Arrive uncluttered with preconceptions; instead, keep your mind receptive and allow yourself to free-fall into a Garden of the Mind. Here at Stanstead Park on the borders of Sussex and Hampshire is a surrealist garden that you'll either love or hate but that, most certainly, you will not dismiss with an indifferent shrug.

Sometimes my first visit to a garden has such an impact that I can never shake it off. Certain attributes remain forever in my memory. For instance, nothing can erase my first impression of the thirty-acre wood at Castle Howard.

Here grow the results of many journeys the late James Russell made to collect seeds from distant lands. Once his seedlings were six inches high he planted them in the wood where they were left untended to spread themselves freely through the undergrowth. The sight of such roses as *R. sericea* or a scrambling *R. pimpinellifolia* in their wild setting remains indelible. Nor shall I forget John Hubbard's garden in Dorset: accompanied by a soughing in the pines behind the house – it might have been waves breaking on the shore, which wasn't far away – his garden entered me intravenously. The impact of the scent and colour of a cloudless June morning, when I'd driven with a friend all the way from Shropshire, has been in my bloodstream ever since.

In the same way, my first impression of peacocks and rust in Ivan Hicks's garden can never be effaced. The absurdity of finding these two in the same act delighted me. Conditioned to think of peacocks belonging to one kind of setting, and rust in another, I still find it hard to get them both in focus. When I arrived I was confronted by peacocks, stately, aristocratic and exotic creatures which in my limited experience belonged to grandeur, lawns and topiary. Some were roosting on the top of a wall where their enamelled throats rose above a tangle of ivy, some were poised motionless on finials, and one displayed his splendour with eye-catching ostentation, appearing as an unexpected prelude to a garden of corroding machinery. The plangent cries of the birds were like ululations from the Underworld as they punctuated our passage along Ivan's metaphorical Journey through Life. 'Liberated imagery' in the form of a trio of shop dummies painted the colour of cloudy skies was reflected in water.

Rusty cowling, disc harrows and anti-invasion spirals –
the kind that lay coiled along the beaches in wartime
– rose from among flowers, but before I could linger to
look, my credulity was stretched even further by fairytale
parables and symbolism. A Tree of Knowledge – a *Malus* –
had twined round its trunks a snake-bark maple. The legs
and hips of two truncated women were sensuously clasped
by coils of laburnum; two Trees of Heaven (*Ailanthus
altissima*) marked the entrance to Paradise, and if you
were to wilt on the way there you could pause a moment
in the Stress Chamber on a seat surrounded by aspens to
soothe you with their whispering.

Ivan Hicks, whose knowledge of trees is boundless, said:
'Why plant one when you could plant three?' Yes, why?
I'd never considered. His method, which would appal any
arborist, is to plant them so close that they grow into a
single unit, strong and bold. 'But better still,' he suggested,
'is to plant five, near enough to merge into a canopy.'
Twelve Leyland cypresses are planted together to form a
dark tower; on the inside all the branches have been cut
off, leaving space for a ladder leading up several storeys.
The tower is entered through a weathered Gothic door the
colour of faded scabious, and from the mysterious interior
you can peer out through the many small panes of a Gothic
window. Elsewhere is a living bridge, made by planting
four oaks at steeply-slanted angles and removing all the
branches except for those that form the hand rails and the
treads. The bridge spans a 'river' of boulders turbulent with
forget-me-nots in spring.

The confusion of legend, reality and surrealism is
punctuated by old rusty iron contraptions, such as an

auger used for boring into wood, shabby office furniture – including a typewriter encrusted with houseleeks – cast-iron drainage covers, contraptions for marking white lines on tennis courts, and hat stands. The garden is restless; things are always on the move as Ivan and his wife Angie chase ideas, re-site objects to make space for a new piece of rusty apparatus, and fight to keep the peacocks from eating the strawberries.

The ripples from his garden form circles way beyond the walls and surrounding trees into the garden designs Ivor makes for other people. But what if he's asked to come up with ideas for what he doesn't like? 'I talk them out of it!' Of course; how simple. 'And anyway, if they've called me in it's because they haven't any imagination of their own or they haven't the time. But sometimes, if they have too many ideas and they're difficult to work with, then I need to hold their hands.'

Is it more than mere coincidence that these gardens – except for Nicole's and Sylvia's – were made by men? Does gender come into it? Or is it that men are adventurous and innovative; they need continually to be challenging themselves to see just how far they can go? Are the tangible attributes of a garden for some men simply elements to be tackled and manipulated, while for others it is the philosophy and the control of cultivation that pushes out the frontiers of their minds? Women, who on the whole don't feel a need for orderliness and for controlling nature, prefer a feckless and improvident approach in their search for freedom. They make romantic gardens amid sensuous surroundings. Is it not the eye of the storm for which they are searching? A calm centre to life, rather than conundrums? I can't answer my questions yet because I haven't seen enough gardens. But one thing is for sure: in France it certainly wasn't women who devised their impressive topiary.

The Unknown Region

The media exude overweening hubris as to how we ought to garden. The inexperienced can find this threatening when their ideas and practice are at rock bottom. But don't be bullied. Begin from the premise that there are many ways to garden. The ground rules are there to be explored; you can do it this way – but you could try the other. Alternatives proliferate, but no novice has the confidence to experiment. Hopelessly wary when I began, I needed a friend to tell me how to lay out a herb garden, what climbers should go against the house and what was the advantage, if any, in growing fastigiate trees. My first attack of clematis wilt sent me berserk.

Because any of us can try anything – some of which may work and some may not – I know now that I can go for whatever I like in a garden. But there's the rub. Supposing you don't know what you like? Suppose you have vague longings so amorphous that your piece of paper, lying beside a collection of picture books and stern gardening manuals, remains a blank? Those who can say 'I know what I want' are lucky, but for those who can't, slow down.

Start from what you do know. If you can only garden occasionally, that already sets limitations. The history of the house may dictate a design, while hideous surroundings can be dynamic persuaders. Salt-laden winds rationalize possibilities, as do gales that savage young trees and shrivel the buds. Is your garden a place for young children? For vegetables? For entertaining, or for privacy? Or is it for those who are mainly housebound? Does it have to be seen primarily from indoors? At ground-level, or from upstairs? Will you one day open it to the public – so that any paths you lay down must be wide and well built enough to cope with hundreds of feet? Or is it to be so personal and concealed that your planting must deceptively hide the boundaries in thickets of greenery?

Once one or two decisions are made other things fall into place, and you will find yourself nudged in a specific direction, whether yours is an urban or a country garden. There's one other restraining condition: your cheque book, which may decisively put the kibosh on the pursuit of foolhardy ambitions or losing your head in a nursery.

For those who go beyond mere wishful thinking, and do take that pivotal first decision to make a garden, the prospect is, without exception, daunting. Nights rendered sleepless by a plethora of information, second thoughts about a tree you've bought, and panic at the great root of something a kindly friend bequeathed you yesterday, are enough to head off an inexperienced gardener into the hills. Instead of your confidence growing, you discover what a labyrinthine subject you have wandered into. Most of us starting out for the first time need a steady current of encouragement. We need people who know more than we do to offer support in the form of a verbal tilth in which to root our determination not to be downhearted.

Encouragement, and then later on the garden itself – like some fermenting nectar – may have carried Michael and me forward when we first began to garden in 1980. But of equal and more sobering value were the times we stood about ruminating. There's a lot to be said for mooching vacantly; it has a leavening effect on ideas. Looking at our putative garden, not just on the threshold of the house but from different angles, and at different times of the day or season, we would discuss and argue until we were forced to return indoors for a book on trees. On wet days when we weren't outside we found that looking from an upstairs window was equally revealing. If you view your garden from a higher level, something that you may have been feeling was never quite right but didn't know how to remedy can suddenly be solved from that aerial perspective.

With the current trend for 'outing', I'll come clean: for me, flowers are the last resort. But before owners of the nineteen million gardens of Britain recoil in horror, I'll explain. When you've run out of ideas, plans for bulky greens, constructions, hard surfaces, water, statues, drystone walls, textures, verticals, benches and follies – and of course shrubs and trees – it then might be the moment to think of flowers. They are the decorative part of a garden, which can be fun, fickle or explosive. Use them for their luxuriant growth and scents as well as their way of surprising you with their ability to soften or outline architecture. I do like their versatility, their power to change the expression of a place. And yet I never feel at ease with flowers. I haven't a natural touch; I don't respond to them intuitively, as I do to trees or bulbs. The theory of how to cope with a flower is in my head, but I haven't done much about it yet. Flowers take over, they get out of control; their habit of running away with what you imagine to be malleable plants is disconcerting. Generally, Michael and I stuck to trees and shrub roses.

'What shall I do next?' asked Lady Jane Grey of those custodians silently surrounding her as, blindfolded, she groped towards the block. The poignancy of that sixteen-year-old's question has stayed with me ever since I first read it. After all, doesn't the same question come up so often in life – though not necessarily under those circumstances? It's certainly one we used to ask ourselves at times when the garden was a wreck and we didn't know what we should be doing.

When you're overwhelmed by indecision, remember that there are no right ways to make a garden. No one will warn you against being stampeded by current fads or by what your neighbours are doing or, worse still, against being pressured by dogmatic advice on how to make a mirror-image of all those thousands of other gardens up and down Britain. You mustn't feel threatened by what you think you ought to do; choose, rather, to go for what you want. As for Good Taste, that overbearing tyrant that sends the inexperienced gardener into a spin – forget it. There is absolutely nothing intrinsic about good taste in gardens: it's as fickle as fashion is when it dictates whether bosoms are in or out, or trousers should have turn-ups. If you want a gnome leering round marigolds, why be coerced into following tasteful pictures in the glossies?

Instead, experiment. Please, do. If you have the slightest

hankering to be deviant, surrender; if your mind's-eye garden is as greedily overstocked as an improbable cornucopia, put it into practice. It's hard at first, as we found, to have enough confidence to follow an unorthodox idea with plants or in design, but in the end you may find you've made something resplendent; something that really startles you with its originality. To hell with rational discrimination. If your heart is set on floral gluttony, try it – anything, and if it doesn't work take it apart and do something else.

Gardens are the most forgiving areas of life you'll come across. Relationships aren't: they can't be transplanted, manipulated, intertwined or cut to the ground with the confidence that they'll sprout again. But gardens can.

And remember: nobody knows what you *haven't* done. Suck on that fact like a soothing throat pastille, and keep mum.

Women who come to gardening only once their children have left home may find their horizons expanding in a way they'd never dreamt was possible. Having given out to others in one way or another for years until they felt laid waste, they at last find a place of their own. A garden is somewhere to be as solitary as they want, with all the peace and freedom to make their own decisions, and where they aren't continually being got-at. A garden is private: no one can trespass on space unless invited. And for the first time, perhaps, they are using their minds in a way quite unlike they did in the domestic sphere. For men, too, a garden offers a sanctuary and escape that exist nowhere else in the same way. A friend in Oxford finds that his hours in the garden work for him like a Turkish bath; there may be

shadowy figures in the steam, but as they drift in and out
of focus he feels no compulsion to communicate.

Pitfalls

Years of walking forwards and sliding back have crystallized
my imperatives. If I were starting out again to make a
garden I would have a clearer idea of priorities. Everyone
must have their own. Mine can be taken as either induce-
ments or warnings – at times I was driven to wonder why
anyone in their right mind likes gardening when so much
of it is warfare. The scratches, the stiffening fingers, the
crouching, reaching and kneeling in bad weather all lack
a certain allure, to say nothing of the part of gardening I
loathe most – watering, whether with a hose or can. Both
are impossible. Whichever method I'm using, I always think
the other would be preferable. It never is. The hose kinks
and gets jammed on posts, catches shrubs and sends pots
crashing over. But then, the watering-can plays hell with my
spine, neck and shoulders, leaving me stricken throughout
the following winter.

There were other things, stupid and trivial, which at the
beginning threw me off course. A small warning sticker
stuck onto the order form would have saved a whole
year's frustration when we found that the colour of the
tulips spread across the garden looked nothing like the
tulips detonated across the pages of the catalogue. As
for winter pansies, it took three or four years to cure my

misplaced optimism. I fell every time for their sweet gaiety, forced into flower to coincide with the downward slope towards Christmas. I imagined their feline faces outside the kitchen window, cheering me through the grey days of winter. Instead they died, leaving greeny bits looking like watercress but without the advantage of being eatable. Nor do roses behave according to the written word; it's only with experience that I've learnt their characteristics, and to take with a large pinch of salt any descriptions I read in print.

Gleaning ideas and adapting them for ourselves made up a large part of our early gardening, but so did advice given to us from experienced gardeners who arrived in autumn with clumps of plants from their annual divisions. Thinking it was better to submerge than to be left stranded, we accepted and planted everything with a kind of naïve cupidity, and certainly without any warning of the proprietorial habit of things like loosestrife, scarlet poppies, yellow irises, and lady's mantle with its elegant leaves and lime green flowers. The result was a slight fraying at the edges of our humour when we discovered what we'd done. After the second summer delighted with the results, we didn't remain long in a quandary but dug the lot up. Or thought we had: I still see the loosestrife mistakenly planted round the pond fifteen years ago annually erupting into tough yellow spires.

Early we learned to stay clear of garden centres: the choice there is too much for those whose responses aren't under control, and mine were always fragmenting. At the start we lurched about, first in one direction and then, too easily distracted, in another. Beguiled by the herds of plants displayed at the entrance to a garden centre which were flowering their heads off because they had been force-fed to bloom ahead of the season, we'd arrive home with the car full of pots and without a thought as to where we would put them. It's all so easy, so seductive. The hard sell at these places – at least for the uninitiated – is calculated. If, like me, you find the shelves of washing powder in a supermarket too confrontational, never enter a garden centre. They are a hundred times more baffling.

The truth is that garden centres are not for the ignorant; and when you are no longer ignorant, you wouldn't choose to go to one anyway.

The best place for buying plants is a nursery that has none of the soliciting-to-buy and the gimcrack tat you have to negotiate in garden centres before you even reach the plants. And if the nursery is part of a garden in which you can see for yourself the plants that are for sale, that is perfection. Nurseries like these are on the increase, and they are worth finding because in every season you can see what you are on the point of buying in its true state. And as more and more private gardens which open to the public now have plants for sale, there's an added bonus to garden visiting.

Golden Rules should be nearly always broken (my mother taught me that quite early on in my life), but it was some time before I realized that this applies nowhere more frequently than in a garden. Many horticultural rules can be stood on their heads: because I forgot to prune when I should and pruned when I should not, my plants blossomed out of step. A daphne, having been shorn at the wrong time, flowered prodigiously in midsummer. Contrarily, when I sheared back a ceanothus after flowering till the limbs were stark enough to make gardening experts wince, this savage treatment had a miraculous effect. Invigorated, the ceanothus produced pinhead specks of green in August which by September had thickened into a green fleece promising six weeks' flowering next May. When I have followed the rules and pruned a buddleja in March, for instance, I've killed the thing. The book I used for practical gardening was never so practical as to say, 'Take no notice of dates: this operation depends entirely on where you live.' I shortened the lives as well as the branches of several buddlejas before I had the sense to wait six weeks beyond the prescribed date. And we soon discovered that nature herself doesn't play the game: frost-tender cistus, pittosporums, magnolias, crinodendrons or teucriums can sail through bitter weather with stoic fortitude – or they may be felled overnight in the same neighbourhood. Countless times I've discovered that something I've cut down to base has next year astounded me with its tenacity for life. Stricken plants that have been written off are quite likely to revive, as I have recently found out, to my shame. Unable to dig up a pittosporum that I had assumed was dead, I chopped off its limbs and planted a jasmine to climb up and hide the dismembered remains, only to discover in June, to my delight, that the shrub was putting out new leaves. Sorry. I felt a beast – I still feel a beast, and now every time I pass the pittosporum struggling back to life I avert my eyes to avoid being overwhelmed by justifiable guilt. By next summer, presumably, it will be back to some sort of shaggy familiarity.

Had we looked from the beginning at what did grow

well in our locality, we might not have been tempted to go against the grain of the garden. Grow what works. I've learnt that now. And if I'd learnt it at the start and seen how winter jasmine thrived in our area but that there wasn't a magnolia around for miles, I might not have expended time and money on those unsuitable trees. Nor did I pay enough attention to the bearing of a plant: how some drape and flow with agreeable pliancy in contrast to those with a rigid demeanour. How easy to get it wrong. Garden manuals have hieroglyphics beside plant names denoting soil condition, tenderness, evergreens, et cetera – but never stance. Height and season, colour and scent are listed, but not deportment. Some shrubs curtsy to the ground while others have skeletal legs which need concealing at the base with bits of floral twinery. Roses in particular are devils for this; their naked lower limbs aren't something to be celebrated, so now when I plant one I surround it with lavenders or santolinas – plants that aren't showy enough to detract from the rose but which conceal bare branches and also act as a solid plinth to relate the rose to the earth. In fact, I like this way of growing a rose so much that I try now to put in something silvery-grey from the start.

Minor setbacks may be part of the rich tapestry of life in a garden, but at times the tapestry can appear a bit threadbare. When I first started I hadn't learnt to take the long view, to be objective and to dismiss failures. Each disaster felled me. Crushed, I took every death to heart and mourned with a kind of humourless and grim fatalism.

But gardeners learn very quickly to accept death with equanimity. It's not you who are a failure: a late frost or, even more deadly, a continuous cold wind can shrivel a plant with lethal finality. And this, I'm reassured to discover, happens to every gardener however experienced she or he is. Death is a part of gardening as inherent as slugs. If you're trying to grow a tree (a *Cornus chinensis*) or a shrub (a *Hydrangea villosa*) or a small plant (a *Convolvulus mauritanica*), and it dies on you – I believe you should give up after the third attempt. A gardener living on the coast of northern France taught me this. Once she had discovered what did do well in her garden, she suppressed ambition and concentrated on getting hold of as many varieties of that particular family as she could lay her hands on. In her case it was cistus. The effect of a glut of colour from cistuses with kohled 'eyes', their single papery flowers seen against a grey sea and coastal rocks, needed little else to make this one of the most supreme gardens I saw in France. Her self-control and her acceptance of the climatic limitations can be found at the heart of French gardeners all over the country. Their *tant pis* philosophy is salutory for those of us who have an inclination to wring our hands; it's something I envy and try hard to acquire.

Death can be deceptive, however; only advice from an experienced gardener stopped Michael and me from digging up our bay tree when a hard frost had turned it crunchy brown. In despair we would have got rid of the evidence. It's now twenty feet high and still growing.

The truth is that plants make fools of us. They play 'possum, appearing withered and past salvaging until, one day in spring, we find that somewhere deep down life is clinging on and a clematis or a caryopteris throws out tiny green shoots, causing us to smile besottedly.

Starting from Here

Novice gardeners should allow themselves from the outset the freedom to be as wayward as they want and to follow their instincts, not prescriptions. There really *are* alternatives to having a central lawn bordered by flowers and khaki brick paving encircling a specimen weeping birch. Roses don't need a 'rose bed' – they grow anywhere: up walls, of course, but among flowers, in grass, out of paving, in the midst of herbs. There is a rose for every situation, from miniatures in containers (which I've never grown) to forty-foot sprawlers (which I have, in abundance). Just one shrub rose in a small garden will work; it may flower only once, but then so do bulbs, and you can always grow a clematis to stitch the rose with late flowering whites or wine-reds. Nor is it obligatory to plant things in trios, or for all the largest flowers to be at the back of a bed and the little ones edging the front. You don't have to break your neck to achieve 'all-the-year colour' if you don't want to. You can let your garden slump in winter into browns, greys and black, and enjoy its look of old grainy photographs.

As for the levels you have been allocated, you don't need to accept them. Changing heights make such a fundamental difference that I wish Michael and I had spent more time considering this aspect of garden structure when we started, rather than being preoccupied with trees. We could have been far more dashing than we were. I see now that even in a small garden surrounded by walls, a change of level can make any number of plans feasible: a moat filled with wild flowers, not water; a grassy depression where children and dogs can roll; a circular sunken garden, paved and surrounded by a sweet-scented hedge of honey-suckle, or one of hornbeam severely geometric enclosing heat-loving plants exuding a sense of the aromatic South. The excavated soil could be a bank of spring bulbs either side of steps leading to an upper level of shrubs and a few trees. Construct terraces, a mound, or a small hill covered in euphorbias with a narrow path spiralling up between them. Whatever you choose, you will have changed the facial expression of the garden so that not everything will be seen in one glance from the threshold of the house.

Is it an incontrovertible principle to have wavy lines to the borders? Is it? I must have missed that one. Because someone once wrote, goodness knows how long ago, that it's artistic to have curvy flower beds, you see them every-where. You can't plant a tree upside-down, I agree, but you *can* stand this accepted dogma of flower-bed design on its head, and in ignoring it discover the serenity of straight lines. The worst culprits are owners of eighteenth- or nineteenth-century houses with square or rectangular gardens surrounded by brick walls. To see the relationship of house to garden insensitively destroyed by curvaceous flower beds quite gratuitously laid along walls like these, walls of uncomplicated symmetry, is enough to set anyone's teeth on edge as keenly as it does to scrape one's nails across shiny paper.

The garden is an extension of a house, whether or not it is used, as so often in America, as an outdoor 'room'. Nicole de Vésian's garden in Provence begins indoors; you step from the village street into a large entrance hall spread, not with floor covering of some sort but with huge smooth sea pebbles which carry right through the house to the stone garden beyond. From Gertrude Jekyll's house at Munstead Wood the paths extended in straight lines; they tethered the place to the ground. The garden that I have now is intended to start from the front door. As soon as you walk in you can see right through the house to the garden; on the floor in place of the carpeting that was here when I came, is a path of square terracotta tiles leading to a door into the courtyard and beyond. At first I had pictures hanging on either side of the long hall but I removed them all in an attempt to concentrate on a sense of unity from the inside to the outside.

Straight lines work in harmony with the geometry of architecture. Not only do they reflect garden walls, but they grow from the uncompromising lines of the house. They work so naturally that one's pleased reaction is spontaneous. You don't have to think twice about it. Making curved beds for the sake of curved beds, or making curved paths unless there is a reason for them, takes away a sense of structural repose. But once the grid is in place, mess it up with the ever-changing movement of plants, allowing trickles of those blue, invasive campanulas to leak along the edge of paths, or diascias used like water-colour to blur unyielding masonry.

At Sissinghurst the straight lines are crossed by axes like one-dimensional scaffolding leading to vistas, statues, arches and so on, surrounded by copious plantings. Anne

THERE ARE NO RIGHT WAYS

Scott-James wrote about Vita Sackville-West and Harold Nicolson in her book *Sissinghurst* that 'They wanted a strict, formal design with free, informal planting.' A formal design with informal planting has never lost its validity. If you have no idea how you should begin, follow this long-established formula which still works so well in many contemporary gardens.

A garden needs bulk, some great constructional block, whether of immobile material or foliage. According to where you live, use what surrounds you. Slate or limestone, brick or flint, whatever it is, provides a graphic stability quite apart from what's planted there. If your country is among forests, do as I saw in parts of California, where wood is used in wildly diverse structures. All the sappy smells, the coarseness of bark and the grain of planed lengths were there; knots and burs, detailed bits of bevelling, were used for paths, pergolas, steps, fences, gates, arches and summer-houses. In France hornbeam is used to make arches and seats, but in Britain hazel, being so widely available, would be more practical. Not only does it make wattle fences give gardens a rustic look, but its versatility and its cheapness make it feasible for such instant structures as raised beds full of herbs or openwork fencing for keeping children or peacocks from the soft fruit. Used for arbours, for irregular trellis work, for protection from prevailing winds, or even seats with canopies, its flimsy insubstantial forms give a garden an entirely different character from those where such structures are solid and longer-lasting. Visit a garden without any structures of whatever sort, and you soon realize that something fundamental is missing.

Trees, Walls, Apertures and Water

As for trees, neglect these at your peril. They are the lungs of a garden. Their mass, foliage, blossom, deportment and shade, their density or frail leafiness, their winter silhouettes and frosted twigs and their magnificence and presence are constant, adding a quality paramount throughout the year, remaining long after the lupins have wilted. For me trees are intrinsic, whether commoners or sophisticated rarities; they form the mainspring of a garden, around which everything else orbits. Look at a garden spreading away from under a tree with a straight trunk standing in the middle-ground – whether it's a mature beech or a spindly tree with a domed head – and your eye is carried through the garden to whatever lies beyond so naturally that you aren't aware immediately of why it happens. We tried the effect out for ourselves, tying an open umbrella to a pole and then standing around in different places. This method wasn't exactly high-tech when planning for large trees, but it did help with hundreds of smaller varieties. We determined the positioning of things like our thorns, crabs, plums, rowans and willow-leafed pears by this dicey method, and on the whole it worked – and when it didn't, next year we moved the trees elsewhere.

If trees are the lungs of a garden, walls are the sheet anchor. In past centuries, when labour and material were easily available, walls were an integral part of mansions and

stately homes, manor houses and country estates. Courtyards, kitchen gardens, stabling, loggias, conservatories
and orangeries were enclosed by walls on a scale unthink-
able today. No garden should be without a wall, whether it's
functional or frivolous. We made a few drystone ones on a
modest scale in our wild garden: they were either for sitting
on or for standing pots on. Others were built to support
particularly lax roses that fell about swooning under mops
of pink flowers. Even a small urban garden should have one
wall, if it is only made from breeze-blocks and painted some
cabalistic colour such as that of over-ripe mulberries, olive
paste, seal's pelt, oxblood or raw umber. The things that
can be done with a wall like this vary from making recesses
for pots to having fragments of glass or pottery set into
it in pictures or patterns. Basic and inexpensive, a wall
makes a statement. Depending on the way it lies, it either
brings your eye to a dead stop or else carries your gaze
into the distance. Walls seclude or exclude. Right-angled
walls jutting into a long town garden at regular intervals double the opportunities for planting climbers facing
east and west, or north and south. But above all – the
ultimate provocation – is the sight of a door in a wall.
Opening a door to walk through it is one experience;
closing it behind you is something quite different. Both
are cathartic.

The idea of making windows in your garden shouldn't
be dismissed as whimsical. They're too important not to
consider from the beginning, whether they're openings
as big as doorways or arches in a wall, or contrived from
yew hedging. Used imaginatively, windows, openings, port-
holes and gaps are spatial elements that Michael and I

didn't understand when we first started. They can be so effective. They not only change the focus of a place, but whatever is beyond – messy, unformulated, decaying – acquires its own allure merely by being framed. If you haven't a specimen tree to focus on, with a bit of imagination your debris could be turned into a still-life or a piece of garden surrealism. Even a bunch of plant canes leaning against a shed beside a rusty upturned bucket saved for the rhubarb and a group of frosted pots too decorative to jettison can become worth a second look.

The consummate dimensions for a window are found in what the ancient Greeks called the 'Golden Mean'. It's a ratio of 5 to 3, and whether you make a horizontal or a vertical window, in a wall or a summer pavilion, the ratio is so perfect that once the opening is constructed you never feel tempted to mess with it again, or to cover its intrinsic perfection with a confusion of flowers.

Water is the part of garden construction where you can lose both your head and your heart. Natural water is a godsend, setting a garden off in a particular direction, but there are numerous examples of private gardens without a natural source where it's changed the tempo of the whole place. Water can overflow into ingenuity, humour, lunacy or magic; it's an element that plays with light like nothing else, and at the same time it may engage another of your senses – sound. At the two extremes of the watery spectrum are the discreet spurt and the baroque cascade. Chutes, channels, wall basins, raised basins, dipping wells or dipping tanks can turn a garden around with sound or reflections. But there is no excuse for the owner of a garden full of unusual plants to instal a pre-fabricated shop-bought electric blue 'kidney' in which to plant water lilies.

Illusion and Subterfuge

I'm a phoney. I'm meant to have a garden, yet there are pots of artificial flowers about the house. Manufactured hydrangeas are perfection, with their greeny corymbs and blowzy white flowers. Parchment poppies are so cleverly devised that their crumpled petals almost open before your eyes in naff realism. Anyway, compared to those of a politician or financial gnome, my deceptions are nothing. And one day my grandchildren may find that these exquisitely contrived fakes are as collectable as the kitsch ephemera of the Sixties and Seventies are today. Already those flowers made from tiny beads threaded on wire that used to be put on gravestones in French cemeteries cost the earth when you're lucky enough to find them in an antique shop. If my counterfeit flowers cause some visitors to smell them, it is merely a bit of visual chicanery.

Even when for a time my garden is upholstered in flowers, pure meanness stops me from doing what genuine gardeners do – pick fresh flowers to bring indoors. But to deprive the garden, either on the rare occasions when it's florally abundant or when it's predominantly green and the few blooms are countable, would be unbearable. Instead, a visit to the local market early on a summer's morning to bring home bunches of what other people have striven to grow leaves my garden inviolate. *Other Men's Flowers* is the title Lord Wavell gave his lovely poetry anthology. Oh yes, I'm all for that. I gather the blossoms of other people's endeavours in order to leave my own intact.

The use of plants as a means of harmless jiggery-pokery works in other ways, too. If a house is ungainly, an outlook ugly or a courtyard sunless, plants can be used as a child uses Plasticine. They can be moulded and shaped and used to outwit the eye by their infinite variety of leaves and flowers.

A brick wall facing you out of the kitchen window could have a trellis *tonnelle* making a false perspective, or the wall could be painted with a fantasy *trompe-l'oeil* of Rousseau-esque creatures peering through a Mexican jungle. A more sober alternative could be achieved by using ivy clipped into a tracery against the wall, in geometric patterns or repetitive curlicues. By hiring a drill to make a hole in the concrete paving you could plant a fast-growing 'Dragon Claw' or 'Ivalace' ivy to cut into designs. Ivies have the blessed advantage of being self-clinging – a gardening description I relish in all its deviant innuendo.

Many climbers grow well on north walls; the choice is surprisingly varied. Virginia creeper will conceal a garage, and painted trellis pinned to the wall will instantly change the look of stucco, even before you choose some dazzling things to leap and twine towards the guttering. And why on earth don't more people plant a tree to grow taller than a raw-looking two-storey house? The moment you have a tree – whether coniferous or deciduous – the building will be embraced and integrated into its surroundings in a way no amount of rockery or shrubbery planted along its base can achieve.

In the Palladio theatre in Vicenza is the finest *trompe-l'oeil* stage set where the statues, columns and perspective are enough to fill the mind with improbable deceits. In other situations mirrors have been used in all sorts of ways, not only to reflect a flowery vista. I've seen one used behind the staging for pot plants, so that what was growing there was doubled in number. The mirrored pots looked so real it was easy to be fooled and reach out for one. I think the art of illusion and subterfuge in a garden is under-estimated and under-indulged: it creates fun, light-heartedness, another dimension, and a sense of theatre. And why not? I know there are gardens where it would be unsuitable and wouldn't work, but when you start out, before you lay down the first path, do stop a moment and ponder on deception. You may feel uneasy about it in other spheres, but in a garden there's so much diversion to be had from it.

Fooling with horrors you are stuck with is one of the pleasanter challenges in life. All sorts of things can be used to hide a hideous outlook beyond your garden. Leylandii aren't the only solution. Clipped hornbeam or well-nourished beech hedges grow fast; or a combination of structures (arches, pyramids, pergolas) and luxuriant creepers won't make a hard frontier, but *will* distract the eye from seeing the trouser factory on your boundary. Fruit trees, the common ones, don't only belong to orchards. They are assets anywhere. The high spot of silviculture in a London garden I visit is three crooked apple trees, around which the other plantings of more urbane breeding fit comfortably.

*   *   *

No one should be traumatized by colours. Blue and white gardens are old hat, and silvers have had their day too, but if you lust for vibrant reds, magentas and oranges which theoretically curdle, forget theory. The late Nancy Lancaster, whose garden at Haseley Court was a dream of perfection, mixed strident pinks and spiteful yellows in a way that would have poleaxed the gardening gurus of the past. She liked those colours, she said; she didn't give a fig for good taste – she followed her inclination, and the result was sublime.

The choice of colour for walls, trellis, fences, furniture, pavilions, gates, sheds or pots is critical. It not only sets the humour of a garden, but works as a cohesive theme running through the whole place – or it can be used to make clearly defined areas. But this aspect of making a garden is never given a high enough profile for beginners. Reams are written in books on interior decoration, but what of garden decoration, whether it's as small as a 'room outside', or compartments in a landscape of several acres?

On a raised paved area where I have French lavender, purple sage and pink phlomis, backed against blush noisette roses and the long-flowering clematis 'Ville de Lyon', there's a pretty slatted chair I painted the blue of hyacinths. Violas the colour of damson purée made with a lot of cream share a blue pot with pale pink petunias. The fact that I seldom sit there because the chair is so uncomfy is not the point; the point is that in a small bit of the garden plants, pots and furniture create a piece of theatre. Next year I might change it all.

You still see the same old banal designs of lawns, curves, patio, trios of conifers thrust at the millions of readers of too many garden magazines. How long will it take to loosen that dead hand? Yet something is happening. A gentle horticultural eruption is taking place. In the last five years or so gardening has become more imaginative, sophisticated and adventurous, in a way Michael and I never foresaw when we looked through our first gardening books. The conventional boundaries have been expanded, and designers now use materials and plants with a speculative curiosity.

If you've never gardened before, take heart. There is such a wide spectrum of horticultural temptations available that you're sure to get it wrong. At the beginning, certainly, but later too. Never mind. The charm of gardening is that as everything is forever on the move, you can change and alter things as you go along. Ambitions or aberrations are part of the allure. Go for what you want, not for what you are told you want. Whatever nourishes your impulses should be your launching pad.

It's all too easy for me to hand out these didactic pronouncements now that my gaffes have been littering the garden for years. And they still do. But I don't underestimate the dilemmas of those green gardeners sinking for the first time into a bog of garden manuals and omnipotent rules. If a lot of this chapter sounds bossy, it is. The only comfort for beginners is that some of our experiences might be helpful to those as insecure as we were when we started gardening. Remember, my prejudices are personal and opinionated. What matters is that yours should be too. Anything, anything please, to get away from bland conformity nourished on caution.

CHAPTER II

The Germination of a Garden

Gardens hadn't featured in my life until about seventeen years ago. As a child brought up in London, I absorbed them by osmosis; I never gave them a thought, although above almost anything else I longed, with a kind of anguished intensity, to be among them. Gardens and countryside were places for which I yearned with predictable frequency. Like malaria, the malady periodically overcame me. London was a habitat I found bearable only in fog.

My first memory of being aware of flowers, of their beauty and variety, is of looking at the illustrations in a book I was given when I was seven. The story and the pictures filled my heart with a great overburdening sorrow, the sort that children feel when they come across pity for the first time. All the flowers were people: bold, modest, pretty, flimsy and enchanting, they appeared as waiting-maids, ladies, pages, knights, dancers, warriors and soldiers walking through pages I never tired of reading. Troupes of forget-me-not children played among gardens peopled with flowers preparing for a ball. On midsummer's eve the spring flowers met the summer flowers, when the love-sick Prince, a lily-of-the-valley, was able to dance the night away with the Princess, who was a rose. All the spring flowers mingled with the summer ones, dancing and feasting together. But as the first rays of sunlight fell across the garden, the spring flowers vanished. I couldn't bear it, but nor could I leave the story alone. I loved the book and lamented over it, hardly daring to look at the midsummer's eve pictures, they were so sad. I've never again come across that book, with its green covers, though I often search among second-hand shops. The fable fixed an image of English gardens so indelibly that their story-tale portrayals remain attached to certain flowers, just as Cicely Mary Barker's series of Flower Fairy books must also have done for generations of children.

Growing up in a city meant that when I did have the freedom to wander where I pleased in the countryside, I became fascinated by the powerful renewal of verdancy. It wasn't that in London I was unaware of the potency of spring – after all, we looked down onto the Embankment gardens in the Adelphi, where the regimented lines of pink and scarlet tulips stunted my responses to these flowers for years – but there was none of the lush ebullience of massive leafiness to be seen, only bedding plants and thickets of dusty lilac round the bandstand. The nutty scent of hawthorn blossom passed me by, and although I loved the plane trees of London it wasn't until I saw beech trees in the rolling woods of Buckinghamshire that I read and re-read Kipling's 'The Path Through the Woods', for the *frisson* it gave me, and in the childish belief that he must have been writing about these woods.

My commitment to gardens and to the country took root when I was looking the other way, with the result that my earliest awareness of horticulture was soaked up through my skin, rather than assimilated consciously. Yet my sister, four years older, never had these responses either to flora or fauna, so that I can only think my yearning to be out of an urban environment was as inherent to me as the bias towards politics and sculpture was to her.

Childhood Gardens

When you are not concerned with their maintenance, gardens and the vagaries of their needs have a dreamlike quality which can never be recaptured once you know too much. In school holidays I used to stay in a variety of counties, beautiful ones such as Wiltshire, Cornwall, Norfolk and Dorset (though alas! never in the North, a deprivation I still regret), with either school or family friends. The gardens surrounding the houses varied: some were small and cottagey with old-fashioned flowers and trim little veg gardens; some were large orderly places and others appeared as rambling regions of unkempt-ness. With total freedom and what seemed like limitless time, we played games and dressed up, spending days of make-believe among imaginative deserts and jungles where we invented our own fantasies.

One I remember well was the garden of an ancient priory owned by a Communist barrister with a household of maids, a cook and a butler, a nanny and a chauffeur, and a whole hierarchy of gardeners. Left to ourselves in this enchanted garden that was always sunlit we roamed paths, hid in shrubberies, climbed trees and sidled through gates in high walls. Life was a series of halcyon days where time had no margins. Deep beds of perennials flanked long straight paths backed by espaliered fruit trees so neatly tied in that they formed regimented patterns with not a leaf out of place. And here were butterflies. Oh, those butter-flies of childhood. That everchanging fluttering mosaic of brimstones, skippers, speckled woods, and various whites including the marbled whites with complex grey-and-black markings and the green-veined whites; orange tips, small tortoiseshells and coppers; peacocks, wall browns, holly blues, the magnificent red admirals (they still visit our gardens in autumn); Camberwell beauties, ragged-looking commas, fritillaries (the family is so big I can't remember which were here), painted ladies, swallow-tails and the sensational purple emperor. What chance today for a child to see even a fraction of the 100,000 or so species of moths and butterflies around the world? Fascinated by their unworldliness, we would enclose their ticklish wings within our cupped hands before releasing them on to different flowers to see if they'd return to where we found them. Sometimes, as we lay on our stomachs in the grass, we'd put out a bait of sugar lumps in an attempt to lure them down to our level. Butterflies and grasshoppers have all but vanished from our gardens. I don't suppose any child now experiences the whirring acrobatics of springing insects accompanying each step they take when walking through long grass, or tries to catch a grasshopper in repose.

In another part of the garden, away from the lawns and formal grandeur of topiary and arbours, we could cross the bridge leading to an island in the river. Here among shadowy shrubs we made a world of secret bothies for trysts, hide-and-seek and endless make-believe. Gazing down through the still water of a pool full of lilies with the greenish flesh of leprechauns, we saw last autumn's leaves caught in a web of barely perceptible weeds where small brown fish darted and hovered in the depth. We'd stare intently at our reflections until one of us dropped a pebble, breaking the surface and dissolving our faces in the ripples. Overhanging trees formed green shutters enclosing us as we paddled a wooden punt along the river where swans glided round the island, but after one confrontation we learned to be wary. We were not sanguine when the swans were nesting and we came too near; they were transformed into monsters with outspread wings, hissing with menace. We fled, terrified, from their tumultuous pursuit. The threatening sound of their beating wings followed us back across the bridge to safety. In farmyards we'd been attacked by geese – but swans, so regal and gliding in repose, were far more formidable when aroused.

Another garden that is transfixed in my memory lay in a Gloucestershire hamlet under Bredon Hill. It is long since gone, turned into an antiseptic clone by the usual suburban face-lift so popular in all the leaden garden magazines. One more endangered species has been wilfully uprooted, and every single feature you hope to find in a classic cottage garden has been destroyed. Why do people choose a country setting and then turn it into suburbia? Their over-zealous tidiness makes one wonder what their problems are. Are they the same people who compulsively wash the door handle before turning the knob?

When I used to stay there, the cottage garden was already well-established as a place of mossy fruit trees and dense hedges where birds returned to the same nesting sites spring after spring. No pesticides or systemics had been used, so that butterflies caroused among the flowers and nettles grew along the thatched buildings in the farmyard and along the outside of the drystone wall where white and pink valerian seeded freely between the stones. For about eighty years the garden had remained the same: divided into small patches of lawn and framed by beds of perennials and paths of gravel overhung with nepeta, lavender, campanulas and gilliflowers and shaded by wooden pergolas sagging under the weight of roses. The place was redolent of pinks, lilac, and the pungent smell of rue and cabbagy peonies. At one end of the house, where the walls were hidden by a tangle of honeysuckle and ramblers, was the kitchen garden. Self-seeded aquilegias performed arabesques among rows of greens, root vegetables, wigwams of runner beans and soft fruit bushes whose branches, fossilized by age, continued to produce gooseberries and currants year after year. And every spring without fail stems of delicate pink rhubarb pushed up through the terracotta forcing pots, later to be made into pies with a patty-pan to hold up the pastry crust.

Drystone walls, a wooden water butt, an old iron roller and a thatched summer-house smelling of rust, swallow droppings and the rotting canvas on deck-chairs gave the garden a sense of loving antiquity. The owner, a business-man from Birmingham, had for decades spent his week-ends planting old roses with names that read like poetry. Gardens like these can't be instant. This one had evolved as slowly as coral does on the Great Barrier Reef; its decrepi-tude resulted from devotional gardening and a sensitivity that came from instinct rather than rationalism. Unlike the barrister's large garden tended by employees, this small one was, for children, a place not for make-believe but to come with an armful of books, for dolls' picnics and for gathering posies for the house. The orchards were full of smallish trees whose fruit made the best and driest cider, which the family kept in a barrel in a stone-flagged larder off the kitchen. The cloudy liquid may have looked inno-cent to a first-time visitor, but those who underestimated its potency risked temporary oblivion. From here in spring I used to pick the primroses lying in clumps along the banks. I'd put them into a box packed round with wringing wet newspaper to send to my mother because I felt so sorry for her stuck in London missing the wild flowers. Long before they arrived the water would have turned the box into a soggy mess, but it kept the primroses fresh, she told me. In August, lying on my back in the orchard, I'd hold up a grass and look intently at the design of a blade and seed-head against the sky, something I could never do in St James's Park where my sister and I were sent to play on Sundays.

Besides the Communist's and the businessman's gardens, there were others, remembered more for their atmosphere than for their horticultural variations. I wonder: can you implant a love of gardens in a child? I'd like to think so, although it really depends on the opportunities children have for exposure to colour, light and scents. Then, perhaps, an almost unconscious assimilation can take place, without them necessarily having to play their part in the labouring. Some residue must remain, surely? And there are many adults who not only remember how, when they were young, they graduated from a tray of cress growing on a window-sill to being allowed their own small patch for nasturtiums, mignonettes and radishes, but how childhood gardens gave them a sense of attainment. This unspoken 'feel' for gardens remains with them until, much later in adulthood, they come to make their own places. As someone said to me, 'It was years before I realized that everything I did was my way of trying to get back my memories of childhood gardens.'

Our First Garden

Setting out to make a garden is personal. What finally influences your decisions much depends on your sources. Some people use books, some use professional designers, and some use friends, whose advice can be subjective as well as contradictory. In the end Michael and I found that our friends' conflicting points of view were a great help.

They forced us to clarify our own minds, and by rejecting some advice and picking out the bits we liked, our own taste became less ambiguous and we gradually settled on the priorities.

There are two extreme methods of making a garden. There is the full-frontal approach, as undertaken by two gardeners who designed their place with enviable imagination and precision before ordering one tree or bringing home one stone. For them 'We made a garden' became the most emotive phrase in their language. At the other extreme is our method – that is to say, no method. By surrendering to the insinuating and devious way things happen in life, in whatever field, you may be led to where you had no intention of going. That's what happened to us: a breath on the neck, a hand on the shoulder and we found ourselves approaching gardening from the wrong direction. Neither Michael nor I – unlike our friends, whose unique garden was born from judgement – intended to 'make a garden'. In our ignorance (Michael knew as little as I did) we merely wanted to 'do a bit of gardening'. Instead, we ended up with a yeasty monster that went on rising, absorbing our daylight hours and with its subtle annexation and impossible charm inducing night-time restlessness. A garden? What an issue.

Recently I've been intrigued to watch how an acquaintance who has constantly protested that he has no interest in gardening is imperceptibly caving in. Slowly he's succumbing, almost unaware of what is stealthily ensnaring him, and I can see material proof of his thraldom. It's interesting to watch because it's been happening by subterfuge ever since his neighbours did the dirty on him.

Until then he'd done nothing in the tiny square of space at the back of his house but keep his one hedge in trim. Holly, hawthorn and honeysuckle had made an attractive tapestry of variegated leaves and texture which he kept shipshape by clipping it twice a year into an undulating and irregular serpent. One day while he was out, his neighbours cut down the hedge and put up a high board fence in its place. That was far from neighbourly, and he was justifiably upset. Ah, but it was then the alchemy of gardening began to work. He needed instant greenery, he needed a profusion of climbers to conceal the man-high fence, stark and overbearing. You can guess the rest. Fired by both anger and a determination not to be the loser, he has become inveigled literally while his back was turned. Now it's gardening encyclopedias and catalogues that keep him sparking; he's mad to find what will work and what won't, and he's already talking about a shrub or two to go on the opposite side, to balance the fence. We all know what *that* means. Once started, gardening doesn't let go. What a positive conclusion to his neighbours' act of vandalism.

A Very Rural Setting

Our own beginning was not with gardening, but with farming. The village when we first lived there had neither water nor electricity; every winter we were snowed in, and every spring a young lad walked the beribboned and glossy stallion through our hills to serve any mare that was receptive. It was said he would do the same for any maiden. As the hour and route they were going to take were outlined in the local paper, it was possible to be on the look out for this seminal pilgrimage. The stallion was magnificent, ribbons in his mane and tail; the boy was pretty good, too, with a rosette in his hat. Sadly such activities have changed; science has taken over. Without a doubt artificial insemination is a modern impoverishment of life for both man and beast, and a Hardyesque quality of rural living has gone forever.

Years later, when we no longer farmed, we reappraised the buildings and orchards surrounding us and were enticed into a different mode of cultivation. I wrote about the wild sort of method we went in for: how our ideas were based on the trees and the brook, on walls, roses and bulbs. A stream meandered among alders and ash trees; the orchards had a few towering ancient fruit trees, and sheep grazed in pastures just beyond our boundaries. Here we made a garden without flower beds, since all that was needed in such a rural setting was a form of floral touching-up interspersed with disorder – dishevelled, unruly, lush and tousled. The garden created its own unworldly mirage. Using plants as both ornament and material, decoration and paint, we merely wanted to embellish what existed.

We made a pond, from which sprang a hundred un-expected pleasures. Not only from the kingcups, irises, primulas and other waterside plants which thrived and multiplied till the banks were dense with flowers, but from the wild life. Damsel flies, water skaters, frogs, newts, moorhens, dippers and kingfishers appeared with startling immediacy. In March the pond was alive with the sound of mating. The creaking song of frogs lasted for only a few frenzied days – an undignified arrangement – but while it did the heaving fecundity sent the cat wild. She peered into the pond, perilously leaning over while dipping a paw in her effort to catch one creature out of the seething bedlam. Next minute, alarmed by their racket and by the touch of water, she sprang back, only to return to the edge again where she spent hours in predatory frustration.

To make a reader interested in something they've never before considered in their lives, an author has to write so well that the beauty and flow of his or her prose carries you on in spite of yourself: I've no doubt that if Virginia Woolf had written the New Linked Life Assurance Business Annual Statistics, I could become riveted to them. I've never fished in my life, but I read and re-read parts of *The Secret Carp* by Chris Yates – an intriguing piscine fanatic whose paradise lies in shadowy depths – describing the sense of otherness to be experienced when staring at water.

The air is utterly still and a pallid vapour hangs motionless over the water. For eight or nine hours [and he means this; he remained all night in his quest for carp] this stillness has been building like a wall around me, yet the lake has never once been absol-utely flat calm. The pale moon looks static in the west, but its reflection slowly spins and sways like a wobbled plate. There is a constant, subtle shifting, like a gentle sea swell, a just-perceptible undulation. Unlike a small pond or pool, which remains completely still on a windless dawn . . .'

A stillness such as this transformed the farmyard where we made our pond; in the moment before the sun was high, a family of moorhens would paddle among the leaves lying at the water's margin. Their surreptitious movement was impassive compared to the mercurial flight of the kingfisher at midday.

Looking down on a garden from a height can be a revelation. People with verandas and terraces see their gardens differently from the rest of us who are stuck at ground level. A bird's-eye view adds a new perspective on the quartered heads of some roses and on the weightlessness of the single-petalled ones when seen from an unusual elevation. It was for this reason I had a tree platform built – reached by a couple of wooden flights, and with seats for two – thirty feet up among alder trees along the stream. I envied birds; I wanted to look down on our garden, particularly in fine drizzle when colours are more intense, or gaze through the leafless twigs on still days in winter. Within the enfolding shadows of summer and autumn foliage we viewed the paths and roses as the seasons turned. On a specially contrived tray we could haul up a bottle of wine that had been cooling in the brook till evening, and the slightly swaying trees enhanced our intoxication.

Politicians are supposed to have knee-jerk responses to certain topics, and I think we experienced our own form of knee-jerking. Something would catch our eyes or ears with such impact as to cause involuntary indrawn breaths. Hearing the song of a dipper singing on a stone in the stream at the end of the yard could do it, as could the shrill cry of a kingfisher. Tiptoeing to the window, we'd see the bird splinter the surface of the pond before alighting on a twig we'd stuck into the bank just for him.

Another thing that elicited an involuntary response from us was the *Clematis armandii*. Since anticipation is half the fun of gardening (and, sadly, it can often be the best bit), I think that this clematis, which doesn't have a high profile in the indices of gardening books, needs a boost. It's a climber that should be planted for the sheer excitement of its foreplay. Long before flowering time Michael and I would be in a state of eager suspense, waiting for the sight of its bronzy young leaves maturing into glossy green leather. The climax comes on some improbably dismal day when the tight round buds start to open into something unbelievable. The flowers are as far away as possible from the frailty of English violets: they pertain more to the East, with waxy petals that open into single creamy flowers and a smell of freshly-baked sponge cake. This clematis belongs to winter, although usually it didn't flower for us until March or April (In this fickle and precarious climate ours once flowered in February.) 'Apple Blossom', which I haven't grown but have seen in other gardens, has a warm pinky tint to the underside of its petals. Our *armandii* was 'Snowdrift' and it reflected its name one year, when there was snow piled up at its feet against the house where the clematis, already reaching to the eaves, had tangled with honeysuckle and the thorny embrace of the rose 'Madame Caroline Testout'. These two masterful climbers were a godsend; they protected the miraculous winter performance of the *Clematis armandii* – susceptible if planted on a sunless aspect. Why is it too often ignored when really it should be celebrated? Why isn't it more popular? Do tidy house-owners feel threatened by insinuating filaments getting at the guttering? Are they fearful for their spruce and newly-built houses, being got-at by snaking arms and hungry roots? But unadorned walls are a gardener's canvas. Enclosed by a caul of tendrils, or insulated with evergreen climbers, they offer the gardener another dimension.

Clematis armandii was ideal to arouse our responses in winter, but in summer nothing quickened them as instantly as the rasp of whetstone on steel when Michael sharpened his scythe. Scything was a seasonal ritual he looked forward to every year: the early hour, the worn feel of the balanced wooden handle, the curve of the blade, and the sharpening undertaken with unhurried movement to avoid carelessly snagging the edge, were rituals he loved above all others in the garden. The long *shoosh* of the blade through grass, the way the grass folded in wave upon wave of green silk, the instant release of sweet fresh scent, and the rhythmic swing of the scythe, were to him the epitome of August.

Early Summer Mornings

Although Tolstoy's description of scything performed by bonded peasants was written a century ago, it could still apply to Michael alone in his orchard in the 1980s. In *Anna Karenina*, Constantine Levin rose early to join the peasants at their work. Forty-two men followed each other

in a long straggling line, some with coats on, some

in their shirts, each swinging his scythe in his own manner . . . Now, in the hottest part of the day, the work did not seem so hard to him . . . The scythe seemed to mow of itself. Those were happy moments. Yet more joyous were the moments when, reaching the river at the lower end of the swaths, the old man would wipe his scythe with the wet grass, rinse its blade in the clear water, and dipping his whetstone-box in the stream, would offer it to Levin.

. . . The bushes by the river where the grass had been cut and the river itself with its curves, previously invisible, were now glittering like steel; and the people getting up and moving about, the steep wall of yet uncut grass, and the hawks soaring over the bare meadow, struck him as something quite new.

Despite the translation, I find that Tolstoy's description brings back memories of early-morning scything more vividly even than Clare Leighton does in the lovely piece she wrote in her book *Four Hedges*. Although thousands of miles from Shropshire, he catches an atmosphere which pervaded a summer morning when swathes of grass were spread across a meadow. If literature can evoke a smell, then one can almost catch that scent of fresh herbage from Tolstoy's prose.

Because we had choosen to work the way we did, grass-cutting was of paramount importance to the look of the place. Our garden would have appeared as slovenly as an unmade bed if the unifying green (however coarse and full of so-called undesirable flowers it was) hadn't had the illusion of serenity that comes from groomed grass.

A garden like this, without the formality of flower beds, was dependent on appearing slightly dapper. Neglect it, and everything fell apart; it lost its cohesion. As the effect was integral to the design, Michael's method was to closely cut by machine paths winding through slightly longer grass while leaving wild patches to seed. And it wasn't until August that he could assuage his impatience to start on the mowing. Early one morning he'd look outside and, with a sense of liberation, he would take down his scythe.

Summer Evenings

Compared to dawn, summer twilight in our garden had an almost hallucinatory quality. There was an unreality about it unlike that of any other season, except perhaps for the garden under falling snow. With my mind hanging loose I could at times easily have believed there were seraphs lurking in the roses. Those roses were so voluminous that they appeared to go walkabout from one summer to the next. However, the proliferation wasn't a bit of wizardry; it was far more prosaic. Because I was unable to throw healthy-looking prunings on the bonfire, I used to stab cut-off stems of shrubs or ramblers deep into the ground at random. To my delight and dismay, they took root. The earth was so nourishing that months later I would be surprised to discover that a twig of *Rosa longicuspis* was well established in an unsuitable hole beside the old duckhouse, or that a glut of 'Kiftsgates' were sprawling promiscuously in improbable places. As for the 'Rambling Rector', it lived up to its name and was by far the most productive of the lot. My casual propagations have left 'Albertines', 'Complicatas', innumerable 'Rambling Rectors' and many others all over the garden for my daughter to cope with. (I still carry on this vice: even in my small town garden too many 'Blush Noisettes' twine about here and there.)

If on summer evenings it took only a slight change of hour and of light to charge the moment with mystery, tipping us over the edge from the rational to the supernatural, it also took only a moment to tip us back again when we discovered sheep had invaded the garden. Shocked into the real world, we raced to round them up before too much damage had been done. Then, for that moment as we piloted them out, I empathized with the Pakistani cricket supporter who, watching his team lose an international match, shot first his television set, and then himself. But the feeling didn't last once the sheep had been returned to the field. The grouping, the massed bunching of a flock of sheep when the sun is low and they stand in each other's shadows, adds to the pleasure of a garden seen flowing seamlessly into the surrounding fields. On moonlit nights their fleeces reflected light like those in the pictures of that visionary artist, Samuel Palmer.

When I first read this description of sheep I found it so vivid I copied it into my Commonplace-book. It comes from *The Unwritten Places* by Tim Salmon, who accompanied Greek shepherds as they brought the flocks down from the high pastures before winter.

It was beautiful in the sunlight. The flocks moved

like one elastic fluid body, lining out in a single file, coagulating into ovals or circles, fanning out in a vee like wild geese in flight, opening and closing but always remaining one body and covering the ground surprisingly fast, with the black figure of a man somewhere in their midst.

Unruly Flowers

Plants with a peripatetic tendency – such as lamium, loose-strife, soapwort or snow-in-summer – can ruin a friendship. Before I knew better I used to accept clumps of these, the donors never warning me of the consequences. I might just as well have been offered itching powder. These plants are among the most impossible marauders to eradicate. If as you start to make a garden for the first time you are lured by the cool froth of white flowers among grey foliage and by the name 'snow-in-summer', learn from our experience and treat the plant with circumspection. Be prudent: otherwise its nomadic tendencies commit you to an everlasting jihad.

We never fussed about the wild flowers that seeded everywhere. They were as pretty and decorative as any-thing we deliberately brought into the garden. There were exceptions – plants which we despaired of ever controlling, such as ground elder and huge and handsome butter-burs that choked the brook in places. But wind flowers, celan-dine, dog's-mercury, scarlet pimpernel and so many others were left to behave like migrants about the place. As for feverfews, bitter to taste but said to be good for headaches, they were the tom cats of the garden: they prowled, smelt bad, and dissipated their progeny round the garden in a most lackadaisical manner. On a part of the land where the brook cuts deeply through the orchard, which in spring is covered with a nebula of wood sorrel, are field daffodils more glaringly yellow under a leaden sky in April than when yawning at the sun in May. Closing the curtains at twilight I was saddened to shut out those aureate flowers blooming their heads off; waking in the night, I thought of all those throats still open in the darkness.

Certain flowers that project an affinity with other times and other things are so traditional, so ingrained that it's hard to be objective about them. Foxgloves, pinks and penny-royal epitomize cottage gardens and nineteenth-century water-colours in the same way as a Madonna lily is associated with the Archangel Gabriel, or alpine gentians with St Bernard dogs. Hollyhocks traditionally belong to cottage gardens, yet they are so magnificent that I believe there's a place for them in almost every garden. They are vagrant flowers. In a narrow street in the town where I now live they grow in cracks at the foot of a wall, having escaped years ago from the confines of an enclosed garden. On an island off the west coast of France feral hollyhocks reach the eaves of cottages colour-washed in pale blues, pinks and yellows which the shadows cast by towering pines turn to indigo, grey or caramel. At a height of seven or eight feet, the flowers' comely presence transforms the street into a set for a musical.

Unfortunately, though I encouraged them for several

years, hollyhocks never strayed through our garden. As often as I tried, I couldn't get them to grow. Yet they would have looked wonderful against the stone walls or assembled in statuesque groups to counterbalance hillocks of shrub roses. And though I really prefer single hollyhocks, I do see that the double frilly pom-poms have a vulgar and extravagant luxuriance about them that is as fulfilling as a fruit parfait. We may think of hollyhocks as benign in their rinsed tones of fleshy pink, blush white, lemon yellow, maroon or lavender, but don't be fooled. Put your eye to *Althaea rosea nigra* and be drawn into a world the sombre colour of blackberries. Or discover that there's nothing submissive about those with florid hearts. Their demeanour appears docile, but look down the crinkly funnel of a newly opened crimson flower to face the true meaning of voluptuous. You can almost hear the flower throbbing from the effort of breaking out of a bud as round and hard as a bullet.

But gardeners seeking smaller hollyhocks, to avoid either the chore of staking them or having the flowers keel over in a wind, are missing the point of such stately additions to a garden. Why not try petunias instead?

Moods and Weather

The mood of a garden is never defined. Yet it's as integral as design. There are gardens where you move from one spirit of place to another; where, if you are cruising rather than pacing, you become well aware of the changing humours. They come about not only from the garden itself, but from the weather. Weather and the time of year affect its temperament with unequivocal power. Familiar with a garden that I've visited all the summer, I've returned in autumn on a day of mist and ochreous light to find the whole pitch of the place has changed. The seasonal variations that take over our gardens lead us into unexpected responses. The mood of a dewy garden in transient light at midsummer is utterly different from that of bosky verdancy it settles into on a day of gentle rain. The mottled shadows lying across summer lawns when fully-opened flowers are a breath away from shedding their petals is at odds with the tranquillity of stark winter outlines. Illusion and visionary glimpses; water, mist and snow; resonant colours and fragrance, all are germane to a garden's mood – and as far away as can be from slug pellets. It's easy to be 'In vacant or in pensive mood' in someone else's garden; it's in your own that the test comes.

But oh, hell, the weather reports. As gardeners we need to listen to the daily bulletins, yet the gobbledegook they use for something factual, scientific and practical is sometimes beyond belief. Clouds seem always to be 'bubbling' or 'cropping' – and how can snow 'fizzle' out? Are we all infants that we need to be told there will be 'dribs and drabs' or 'spits and spots' of rain, or that every spot is 'odd'? 'Odd' is clamped to 'spot' in the same way as 'nice' is welded onto a 'cup of tea'. As for 'wall-to-wall' sunshine, when I hear we're in for that I immediately visualize a bathroom I once saw where the carpeting went up the side of the bath. In winter, when we expect cold as a matter of course, why does a sharp spell of it become a 'snap'? The use of the word is misleading: snow and ice can often move stealthily.

Not one of the forecasters, whether on radio or television, seems able to give us a terse and succinct resumé, which is what we are wanting. Is it too much to ask? We are listening exclusively for hard facts; the information is vital, and we don't need dollops of blather gumming it up. But perhaps more irritating than anything is when, during the summer, we haven't had rain for weeks and the garden is wilting before our eyes: we are promised a wonderful weekend – hurray! For a moment, for one blissful happy second, we gardeners are fooled – rain! Our spirits rise, anticipating relief to plants at their last gasp. The forecaster *must* mean rain. No, of course not. The cheerful pundits always, but always, mean sunshine, hours and hours of it; they use quite different voices when forecasting rain. I don't expect them to be thinking of gardeners, but they might at least be aware of farmers, watching in despair as their winter fodder has to be used before time because the fields are threadbare during a drought.

When I'm feeling really disgruntled I go to commiserate with the nurseryman, Les, who has a stall in the market. He's a mild man; but catch him during weeks of wall-to-wall sunshine and he's beside himself. 'There you are, they're at it again!' he mutters with uncontrolled irritation. 'Talking as though another week without rain is *good* news. Those weather people never think of people like me whose business depends on rain!' Then he adds lugubriously: 'And anyway, no one buys plants when the ground is like rock.' He and I send bad vibes wafting out towards the meteorological boffins with their depressingly jolly forecasts, and part feeling a lot better.

But there is one forecast that always soothes my spirit, and that's the melodious voice intoning the shipping bulletins. I listen early in the morning or late at night, before Radio 4 closes down, trying to follow the course of coastal locations and sea areas surrounding these islands with their litany of fabled names. What a springboard for the imagination; what epic or heroic images fill our half-sleeping thoughts, riding out at sea on a ritual chant of words. Rising numbers of gale-force winds; mountainous seas; the monosyllabic 'good' and 'calm' generating peace as compared to a prospect of stealthy fog with forebodings of invisibility and annihilating silence. There are other shipping forecasts in the day, but who wants them? Only those people for whom they are intended. But at night or at dawn? Then an audience of insomniacs experiences oceanic terrors while lying safe in bed. We trace geography while vicariously drifting through the seafaring elements. The only time I feel sorry for those nations without a coastline is when listening to the shipping forecast.

Once, when we had many cats, in homage to the shipping recital we named them after some of those places. Shannon, Malin, Cromarty, Lundy and so on were reasonable, but we lost our heads a bit when we changed the spelling and called a pair of kittens Silly Automatic and German Bite. And Dogger, a tabby, had a crisis of identity all his life.

In gardens storms are no good – heavy downpours are destructive and the rain barely sinks beneath the surface;

but gentle rain is one of those recurring gifts to a gardener that never loses its value. Some night I'll wake and, through the open window, hear a surreptitious breathing. I listen. The sound is so gentle, a whisper merely, and I lie quiet to hear if it really is what I think it might be. The sound is living; it's of something rustling and stirring just beyond the curtains. A beatific balm spreads through my body and I long for morning when, looking out, I will see every leaf edged with rain drops.

Sunlight manipulates colour. It leaches out the chrome yellow of ligularia that under thunderclouds appears virulently bilious; those unobtrusive anemones crouching in the grass open in unison and form a pool of such profundity they dominate the foreground. But blues fade and pinks turn brown in sunshine, and through almost cataract eyes we used to watch the garden change as mysteriously as the colour of a chameleon does on a rain tree. This light is intrinsic to summer. Any homesick exile from England pines for it with a kind of corrosive nostalgia. This is something we knew well, having seen for ourselves how flowers in other parts of the world are affected by strong sunlight in quite a different way from those in northern climes.

In the tropics the papery floral bracts of bougainvillaea emit billows of magenta and lurid purple inviolate under a blazing sky. So too do the scarlet flowers of the flame tree which appear startlingly flamboyant on the leafless boughs. Rigid platoons of canna lilies soakes up light like blotting paper until their amber, bronze and mustard blooms shine with opalescence, in contrast to the felty flowers of ivory

frangipani that diffuse the light through their dark foliage.
But wild orchids – ah, those are the most miraculous, not
so much for their flowers as for the latent way they grow
in unlikely places. Along boughs high in the tree canopy
they glow with such incandescence we're compelled to
move towards them with the steps of a sleepwalker. As for
jacarandas – surely the most coveted tree in all the world
– they have blossom that opens before the leaves. The
mauvy-blue flowers when seen high against tumultuous
thunderclouds seem almost to have emerged from them,
the tones of cloud and flowers are so subtly related.

The asphodels of Mediterranean pastures have white
petals with reddish-brown veins, giving a smoky-pink look
to derelict land and appearing slumberous compared to
the powerful pink of oleanders. Their effect in a landscape
of olives and cypresses is tranced, almost arcane, whereas
the little poppies of France which flow through fields or
along verges in May become ever more inflammable under
a midday sun. Sunlight opens morning glory trumpets of
Cambridge blue, almost unbelievable in their intensity of
colour. But a river of blue agapanthus flowing across a
Provençal garden looks better at noon in partial shade than
in full sunlight, when the flowers appear slightly soiled.

Some of the best combinations of plants come from
muddled flowers seen in rafts of colour, whether in a
mixed border or in a field of scabious, ox-eye daisies
and delicate red campion (a plant welcome in my garden
any time). The chiaroscuro effect of either is distinct
from the kind of cerebral planting where colours are
carefully co-ordinated and the gardener has control over
what is happening in the beds. Sometimes I did try; I did

intend colours either to harmonize, or to clash so as to set a mood, but at the beginning I failed. (I still do.) Until we knew how plants performed in our own locality, however diligently we referred to books we were more or less doomed to disappointment. From Hilliers' *Manual of Trees & Shrubs* I used to plan some subtle combination of shape and colour but invariably it was unsuccessful, not through lack of application, but merely through mistiming due to ignorance of the climatic vagaries under our hill, a hill that's just too low to be designated a mountain. We soon learned to be fatalistic, to shrug off our failures; and when the carefully arranged presentation of orange lilies against a blue hydrangea or *Ceanothus* 'Gloire de Versailles' miscarried, we nearly always found that inadvertently we'd created something that pleased us equally well.

As with cooking, no one needs to know it was never actually meant to turn out like that. Strange. There almost appears to be a natural affinity between gardening and cooking (as there is between medicine and music). During a conversation, how easily one subject slides into the other. Put it to the test: how many of your friends enjoy both occupations? There are exceptions, of course. One or two gardeners I know – one who does it for a living – are indifferent to eating. And you can't assume that all gardeners want, or are able, to paint botanical pictures of their own flowers, though a lot do – but what surprises me most is the number of people who can spend hours pricking out and deftly potting on seedlings with infinite delicacy and tolerance but protest that they can't sew on a button. Clearly, having the patience for one kind of skill doesn't mean it follows through to others, even if they require the same dexterity. I can't make good parcels, but I love dress-making. A friend is convinced of the therapeutic effect of pruning fruit trees, but tries hard to coerce his wife into cutting his nails – toes as well as fingers.

Frequently when sitting with a companion, surrounded by the splendour of a garden, I find we're talking food not flowers, and from there food slips into travel, with accounts of remembered meals and the produce that grows abroad. I've never been bored by a shared conversation about eating and where it took place. The connection between gardens and food is obvious, but it doesn't always follow that gardeners grow vegetables. Space and energy may be the determining factor, but it may also be that gardeners find it isn't financially worth the trouble, and they end up with a glut of stuff at the same time as everyone else is going through the same superfluity. However, that's lovely for the rest of us who don't have kitchen gardens. We can relieve them of all their seasonal bounty with gratitude.

An Intangible Feeling

A garden is a sanctuary as well as a creation. It increasingly becomes for me both a spiritual and a physical refuge more transforming than I'd ever imagined it to be. There is the particular kind of happiness – never commented on by poets – which comes from seeing that a shrub you'd assumed dead, one day has minute specks of green on an otherwise lifeless stick. And as this occurs more often than you would expect (at least at the beginning, when you're inexperienced), no gardener should pounce in despair to pull out an ailing plant.

This happiness is manifest every time I work there. If I've been sitting at my word processor uncertain whether to go outside or not, it's seldom that once in the garden I don't wonder why on earth I waited so long. Why didn't I press 'Save and Continue' (one of the more optimistic commands on my machine, and certainly preferable to 'Limbo') and come into the garden sooner? The pleasure of being there is instantaneous. Wayward thoughts proliferate; arbitrary and drifting, they thrive like toadstools in a wet autumn. It's as if the actual fact of physically mucking about with earth releases provocative notions – not a Pandora's box of ills, but feckless ruminations. Drugs may work like this, only to a greater extreme and sometimes with dire consequences, but gardens cannot be called dire; they may fell you with disasters, but on the whole their quality is benign and recuperative. And when my word processor repeatedly comes up with 'Disc data error. Retry operation', I know it's probably gummed up with adjectives and protesting at my lack of discipline. Then, certainly, is the moment to turn to the garden for a change of language, a change of mood. I can tell from the way I threw down my gardening gloves the last time I was out there whether I'd been vexed or happy. If the curling fingers are facing downwards, it was the former; if they lie generously open-handed, the latter.

The Spirit of Place

In 1990 I left that garden. If those words sound bleak, I don't mean them to be: they're merely factual. Gardens are places we all have to leave one way or another, though the timing may not be to our choosing – particularly as gardeners always have an eye on next year.

Gardens bloom and decay in a comforting cycle out of our control. Only the trees endure; those serious trees that will take decades to reach maturity and which remain as a legacy for future generations. As Michael and I planted about two acres of broad-leafed trees, I hope that they will stand *in situ* to be enjoyed by others as passionately as we enjoyed their planting and their early growth. We'd walk among the oaks, wild cherries and chestnuts, and speak about the time when they would be tall enough to form green mansions with paths between and, somewhere, a concealed clearing in which to picnic and to lie gazing into the Shropshire sky. Not a sky like R.S. Thomas's, for whom 'To live in Wales is to be conscious/ At dusk of the spilled blood/That went to the making of the wild sky . . .', but a sky of our surprisingly vaporous Shropshire light that makes it appear further off than in other counties. Or so it has always seemed to me since the first time I looked at it almost fifty years ago.

As for the rest of the garden, it lasts no longer than a damsel fly. Our roses, bulbs and yew hedges will be around for a bit, so will the tree platform for spying on the shrubs – but our own way of doing things should not be mourned. No garden can be perpetuated as the original creators made it. And now my daughter and her family live there, and I don't want her to feel burdened by an obiligation to keep it intact. What Michael and I made was ours; now she must simplify and adapt the garden for her children and her work. She's young; we were not. We had the time to mulch roses every spring, to plant hundreds of lily-flowering tulips every autumn, to encroach into the surrounding land with more trees, more bulbs, or just to follow up any scheme that took our fancy. But that was then; and the garden that was so personal and that depended entirely on our shared enjoyment is something that has gone.

People ask me how could I bear to leave it? Or how can I bear to go back there? But I can; I've moved into another space, I'm concerned with other ideas. I've always believed there is a time for doing certain things, and later there's a time for doing something else. It's only when we're young that we feel the pace of life tearing away under our feet as, tied down by children, we imagine we are losing the chance to experience everything in one embrace.

When I visit my family, and Tamsin and I walk outside together, I remember, but I don't grieve; I'm more concerned that, having little experience yet, she shouldn't be tempted to expand the garden before she discovers just what a possessive creature she's dealing with. Michael and I didn't; we had no idea when we started how we'd be taken over. Ask any gardener. They know the blackmailing ability of gardens: how their tenacious grip keeps us in a state of expectation, or in utter turmoil over climatic devastation.

A wonderful and strange thing happened soon after Tamsin and her family moved there. The place had been rented for the four years since I left, and during that time neither the moorhens nor the kingfisher appeared in the garden. But quite uncannily, a few months after she arrived not only did the moorhens return, but so too did the kingfisher. One morning Tamsin heard a piercing cry – instantly recognized – as the bird flew up the brook and turned into the foldyard to alight on a frond overhanging the pond. If you need proof of magic, of the spirit of place that haunts certain gardens, surely this is it? Since then the kingfisher has often returned, and my grandchildren look down from the kitchen window to watch the tiny radiant king of birds with the iridescent plumage waiting for his prey.

If I were now to turn an objective eye on that garden, having left it six years ago, I would say that the stimulus for how Michael and I worked had continually evolved. The impetus had grown between the two of us as we threw out suggestions, each inciting the other to try this or that idea. We worked each other up with our shared fantasies, but at no time did we set about 'making a garden' with premeditated deliberation. Quite the reverse. In the end we acknowledged that it was what the garden had made of us.

CHAPTER III

Surfing the Flower Beds

When I left the country I wanted to take it slowly. Leaving
the old garden meant extricating myself from thoughts
that clung as firmly as goosegrass clings to clothes. I didn't
want them – thoughts like those. I wanted to move on; to
uproot memories of the myriad small flowers on 'Paul's
Himalayan Musk' floating like a burst pillow over the bank;
to banish visions of reflexed petals on the lily-flowering
tulips submerging under a tide of orchard grass, or the
song of the dipper from down the brook.

Thoughts such as these had to be exorcised before I
could enter a new garden, empty-headed, with no residue
and no left-over prerequisites.

Gardens use two languages. One is easy and needs
no translation: it deals with facts and hard advice. The
second is far more notional. Taking inspiration from many
sources, it's only too easy to end up making a garden

that fragments as ideas ignite and the place becomes a series of squibs exploding randomly. A plan from here, a photograph from there, a bit of history from somewhere else, and the place ends up a mess. A sense of unity and balance, recognizable instantly you enter some gardens, is rare. To a few it comes instinctively, for the rest of us it needs working at. A boring garden may be safe, its unity guaranteed; but it will lack resonance and without that no garden is memorable.

Now, by coming to live in a town I had made the 'Lady-Jane-Grey' question inevitable. It pole-axed me with its unequivocal forthrightness. What shall I do next?

Town Gardens

Back gardens are intriguing. In this town there are those of such a personal and undisguised character that a stranger could easily fit the owner to the right garden on a first encounter, so selective or imaginative that there can be no doubt to whom they belong. One or two – romantic, generous and overflowing with rosy profligacy – are consummate. They work in perfect contrast to the unembellished austerity of Georgian architecture.

There are also genuine Plants People, whose knowledge causes the visitor to tiptoe round in silent awe at the owner's apparent forbearance in growing only those exotic trees, climbers, bulbs and ferns that quench his or her passion. One such green-fingered gardener has created a walled slot alongside the house bursting with tropical verdancy from climbers rampant to reach sunlight. In summer, when you feel glutted from too many effulgent patterns and flaming flowers, a green garden like this one acts as a soothing antidote.

Yet, perversely, there are those with more space than most of us own who have such a paucity of ideas that a visitor wanders round the lawns waiting for the garden to begin. Others, where the property has been in the same ownership for years, leave you thinking 'Nice about the view, shame about the garden'. It wasn't that the place didn't sing – it didn't even hum. Some gardens, neat as a pin, manifestly belong to certain people whose house, dress and conversation are equally impeccable. Others still, threadbare of ideas and belonging to those with neither originality nor humour, reflect a sterility of soul so patent you expect the flowers to smell of air freshener.

At the other extreme is a small, east-facing back yard, heavily shaded by high banks with hedges and overbearing buildings – in fact, with every inauspicious ingredient necessary to stimulate anyone to make a garden – that is a box of delights. Step out of the house and you're in a small enclosure so scented and colourful that the lack of view or of sunlight is irrelevant. With judicious choosing the owner has pots and climbers providing her with a flowery retreat for most of the year.

Limitless money thrown at a garden does not guarantee charisma: quite the opposite, it's more likely to turn the place into a well-honed and highly polished possession with a demeanour that is never allowed to become wanton. Seedlings are eradicated, the earth between plants yearly maintains its distance, the same barren circumference never swerves and, in vanquishing the very intrinsicality of gardens – their random wilfulness – any element of wonder is done away with. In fact, I've come to the conclusion that places like these where money is no problem lack the endearing quality of human frailty. The gardens have never evolved; they have not grown out of trial and error, ruminating, or constant transplanting accompanied by self-vilification. As a result they appear boring, and lacking in charm.

Money builds instant walls. Fountains and pools erupt overnight; arbours, trellis and terrace are erected at a stroke, and fifteen-foot trees are delivered by container along with rolls of flawless lawn carpeting. Where are the tentative decisions, the wavering and standing about in an attempt to visualize what will not take place for years? Where are the shared consultations, the anguishing over expense, the scrappy sketches or fanciful doodlings? To me these are the breath of life of gardening. I want that hesitancy, that pushing of ideas across the table to each other on winter evenings, the arguments and way-out schemes of passing visitors generous enough to share their thoughts, however quirky.

There's a lot to be said for gardeners who are besotted, those with a list one way or the other, who can't see further than increasing their tally of viburnum varieties, or who are dotty about oxalis. I don't mean the experts who cherish National Collections of things, but the passionate and dedicated amateurs who would lay down their lives for their orchids or fritillaries. Thomas Christopher, author of *In Search of Lost Roses*, is a rose junkie from the United

States. His quest was as heroic as the one for the Golden Fleece on the far shores of the Black Sea, as he pursued rose-rustling in Texas and the twice-blooming roses of antiquity at Paestum. His account is one of pure devotion. Having found his lodestar – The Rose – Christopher permitted nothing to deflect him from his single-minded addiction.

People like him bring to gardening a breadth of vision, imagination and commitment that exceed the boundaries of rational gardening. They fire us with their obsessiveness. For the rest of us – in our more down-to-earth surroundings – what a predicament it would be to be asked which plant (rather than which book) we would choose to be marooned with on a desert island. A plant would need to last you through the seasons, fascinating you during every aspect of its yearly cycle. The thought is panicky, the solution impossible.

Women Are Different from Men

I realize that it's contentious to generalize about which gardens will appeal to whom, according to gender. But for several years my conclusions have been solidifying from observations made when once a year the town opens about ten or twelve of its gardens to the public. The event, begun as a one-off occasion in 1990, has become so popular that it's now an established date in June, when people can wander from one disparate garden to another. Their incomparability isn't wholly dependent on the personalities of the gardeners but because the town is on a hill. Unimagined horizons were revealed behind the austere façades. Roofs and chimney-stacks, cupola, belfry and gables, never visible from street level, can be seen from gardens within the city walls. Previously unseen views of the valley that runs northwards from the town are disclosed in one; in another, the castle is to be seen from a formerly unknown angle. Through a window in a wall is a magnificent rising slope of beech trees, and from another opening you can look down on a fertile ribbon of allotments which can only be reached through a gate in a side street. On one occasion we were allowed into a garden running down to the river, glimpsed through overhanging willows.

But that's not all; the spin-off from this open day was intriguing. Visitors' opinions on the gardens were contradictory: almost without exception it was men who universally admired the orderly garden whose fastidious upkeep was manifest. A garden isn't a garden to a man, it seems, unless it is packed with virulently bright flowers contained within razor-sharp lawn edgings, whereas women enthuse over gardens that are secret and atmospheric, with a superfluity about the planting. What does this tell us about our libidos? Put the theory to the test as you go on a tour of Open Gardens next summer: you'll have no difficulty in guiding whoever accompanies you to the gardens that will raise their pulse-rate.

This open day also underlines what I found out a few years ago when I went to judge gardens in a small country town – there's no 'right way' to make one. Some were no more than backyards which, by clever contriving, had been filled with colour. The personality of each owner shone through, whether there was a raised pond no bigger than a bath with a ladder giving access to frogs or a bed flowing with fuchsias. One garden was dedicated entirely to birds; shelter, berries, bathing and foliage for nesting were the mainspring of the design. Another was a tidy kitchen garden where the flowers were grown in regiments among the vegetables, solely for cutting for the house. And one, unorthodox and eccentric, was in the main street, built on the roof of the newsagent. The only access was through a window, but a galaxy of pansies, euphorbias, pelargoniums, two silver birches and a variety of vegetables planted beneath festoons of trailing greenery brought every passerby to a standstill yards down the street. In the evening, when watering was taking place, it sprinkled the pavement and anyone unfortunate enough to be walking underneath at the time.

The variety of taste and individuality made the task of rating one garden before another invidious. Each one was a celebration of the creator's personality.

A Tendency to Waver

I'm more of a contriver than a gardener. When I came here and took over a ready-made garden, I didn't tear it apart. Before undoing everything my predecessor had done – not because she wasn't an extremely experienced gardener, but because I wanted another sort of creation – I paused. For a year I lived here, watching to see how the shadows of neighbouring houses fell. The area stretches towards the east for about seventy yards by thirty. I needed to know where trees should go in, which bits of the garden were permanently in shade and, in winter, where any sunshine briefly fell. I let my thoughts marinade for months while I mentally fidgeted with a jumble of schemes. As each emerged it seemed more lunatic than the last.

One was inspired by a Moghul garden. Would a long and narrow channel running the length of my land work? At intervals there could be shallow water flowing over scalloped shapes with, half-way along, a small decorative pavilion with lacy fretted lattice beside a pool the shape of a square imposed on a circle, as I had seen in Rajasthan.

Another option would be to make a series of brick half-walls, with finials on each concave pediment, either side along the length of the garden. In this way I'd double the amount of wall space for climbers, facing both east and west, and at the same time create small micro-climates for individual plantings. Or should I forsake all that cerebral stuff and indulge my love for roses once again, upholstering the whole place with abundant mounds and forgetting about design altogether?

Alternatively, it would be interesting to set all the plants down the centre of the garden, both the low and the tall ones, with a path running round my boundaries. This would give me a chance to keep the frame of the garden as an uncluttered passage, serene and bare, along which to walk, with only a few selected plants growing up the walls, and with places to sit, each one having its distinctive design and reason for being there. The path here would be of paramount importance: what design and materials I used would be chosen carefully. I might not be able to recreate polished terrazzo, as in Italy – anyway, how unsuitable it would be in this country – but bricks laid on their edges, hexagon or diamond patterns in stone with infills of sea pebbles, or knapped flints as lustrous as oyster shells, could make the path surrounding the plants a thing of beauty in itself.

On the other hand, the reverse kind of garden might have an allure: planting the whole area in floriferous density would render the dimensions invisible. A visitor entering for the first time could be duped into thinking it went on forever. In the centre would be a raised kiosk with vertical iron bars in the openings – unembellished and geometric – in contrast to flowers washing like waves against its foundations.

Another thought: could I have a giant bridge spanning my back garden, as an alternative to having to run upstairs and lean out of the bathroom window whenever I wanted an aerial view of the design? There would be a seat built into the balustrade on the bridge where with friends I could enjoy a new perspective and make notes on everything that was wrong.

I've been half in love with green gardens for years. Is this the time to make one? Decorative leaves and layers of foliage are the primary living elements, paving and artefacts the inert. Topiary and pleached trees make severe designs where the composure is almost palpable and holds its supremacy throughout every season. The French are masters at it, and here the dimensions

I have are perfect. So why not? I hadn't the courage, that's why.

Levels are cardinal features, whether the garden is small or of many acres. I don't mean just slopes, I mean those constructed, well-defined levels where there are steps; where the garden appears as one thing viewed from above, and quite another when seen from below. This sort of design could well suit a back garden, a blessed variation to those conforming to the central-lawn-bordered-by-flower-beds, a formula as depressingly commonplace as chefs in restaurants who dump your vegetables in the sauce surrounding the meat, rather than serving them in a separate dish.

Playing mental games with a JCB is potent stuff – as long as you have access to the garden. Even a smaller, manual digger is a pivotal tool when laying down the design. By reshuffling the earth I would make a sunken garden reached by a few stone or brick steps. I'd use those plants that like to be at the base of things or that are vulnerable to wind. Others needing full sunlight and good drainage could grow on the surrounding banks and terraces, topped by whatever chimera took my fancy. What should I do about paving, an elemental ingredient to any garden?

Dusty answers followed my questions, while my thoughts seethed as actively as frogs in a pond. I enjoyed the indecisiveness; I liked waffling and sinking down into each plan with all my heart. It was mad, heady, and didn't matter a jot because when I rose to the surface again I knew I wouldn't undertake any of them. Taking on a new garden at a snail's pace – no, even slower: at a dead stop – allowed for self-indulgent fantasy, something that has a lot going for it, particularly when you see clones of banal gardening proliferating in every direction. Frivolity is a great healer; it's imperatives that are the killers.

The choices, when you are restricted to a town garden, are infinite – even though I couldn't get a JCB along my hall. They are far more provocative and versatile than we had found them in the country, where the folding land already dictated our momentum and laid a restrictive hand on any foolish ideas we had for confronting nature. But here? I imagined so many totally improvident but equally scenic gardens each briefly enjoying my commited devotion, and I wanted to achieve the lot. Naturally I didn't. Not one. But heavens! the fun of imagining. Gardens in the mind are a branch of insanity, volatile yet harmless.

Faced with the formidable decision as to the design, I'd learnt to remain steadfast to what I wanted, rather than take on someone else's preferences or be intimidated by fashion. No one breathes confidence into you at the start, not enough at least, but by now I knew it was possible to ignore media directives.

So I waited. For a year I did little but stand about, musing. I knew for sure that whatever I did do finally, trees would be paramount. How could I live without those? And as there was not one serious tree in the garden when I moved in except for a holly and an elder at the far end, in my mind trees took precedence over every other consideration.

What bulbs, if any, had my predecessor planted? Which roses were there, and how would they deport themselves?

What colour was the lilac? What should I cherish and what should I banish? I needed time, too, to work out where to sit. As the seasons turn, certain seats remain indispensable while others become too shady, too sunny, or face a boring buddleja before it comes into flower and is covered by butterflies. I've long acknowledged the fact that real gardeners never sit – well, not in their own gardens – which you can prove for yourself when you next go to a friend's garden. Have a look. Count. It won't take long. If they are among the top flight of gardeners, you'll be lucky to find two seats. The best gardeners never sit unless they're somewhere else. Here I have five sitting places for different times of day or year. Benches and chairs are as monumental to my garden as other structures – they are far more critical than flowers, which I can mess with every year according to my mood. I don't mess with the furniture. It's as fundamental to the garden as earth. Benches have supremacy at certain places, where their appearance is important and their dimensions are useful for books and cups as well as humans, whereas single seats can be shifted towards the sun, brought close together, or carried about for shelter or solitary sulking.

The Woman's Gone Mad

In 1991 I began. There are many ways of dealing with space, and I felt I was on firm ground by starting with a path – a direct one. I wanted it to begin at the front door, to run straight through the house, through the glass-paned back door, across the courtyard, under a double oak arch and set an uncompromising line down the garden to where steps would lead up to another level. From there, looking back, I'd have a view of the garden. To add to the illusion of distance, the path narrows by four inches; the steps narrow; two arches are foreshortened; and in my boundary, to create perspective, I have a five-foot-high door going nowhere.

From the courtyard a raised flower bed was removed, made by the previous owner along the base of a magnificent twenty-foot-high drystone wall. The wall is much too good to be concealed with a flower bed and greenery. There is an innate pleasure in seeing one stone plane meeting another at right angles, as you find in Mediterranean courtyards. Away too went the floor of precast concrete slabs, to be replaced with cobbles, setts, old tiles and a herring-bone pattern of bricks. The satisfaction of being able to see the structure of a garden is crucial, and when it is as geometric as this one (even though on such a small scale) the harmony between plants and materials is inherent. As though growing from out of the wall are three stone basins from which a trickle of water falls gently from one to the other. My son-in-law Zenon, who is Greek and accustomed to valuing water as an indispensable element of life, made these for me. In the bottom of a Greek amphora, hidden under a pot of verbenas, pansies and petunias, a small motor recycles the water.

The continual trickling sound is cooling as we sit at a table for breakfast during the months of summer. The early morning sun streams in, lighting up dewy leaves and

half-open clematis buds, melting the butter, and baking
the earth in the pots. By midday the courtyard has become
too hot, and lunch must be eaten elsewhere. Zenon's
basins aren't only for us – the birds use the water too. At
the end of the year, when all the town gardens are parched,
I watch the birds from the kitchen as they preen and
flutter their wings in the water. Having not seen or heard
a song thrush all through this last spring, and feeling sadly
deprived of a bird we'd always taken for granted singing
round human habitation, I was thrilled when one came
to the bath. The thrush's speckled breast and unobtrusive
colouring were almost camouflaged against the stone for
the ten minutes it spent splashing and grooming itself.

Against the wall, planted in gaps at its base, are the
usual things: a ceanothus, clematis, rose, honeysuckle
and solanum. Some have worked, some have moped,
and I have no idea why which did what; but for weeks
each year the wall is densely blue from a ceanothus,
C. × *veitchianus*, growing out of an impoverished hole
and interlaced with a yolky-yellow 'Maigold' rose. The
colours are sublime.

Less sublime are other things. And I move those constantly. Plants, except for certain ones – peonies or
Japanese anemones, for instance – seem most obliging
when ousted and relocated somewhere else. Viburnums,
daphnes, hydrangeas, cistus or lavender – whatever it is –
I find that this somewhat haphazard garden is continually
in motion. Replanting something you've put in the wrong
place is not as dire as it sounds. Five times in four years
I've shifted an Irish yew because I couldn't find the
right position for its black presence to form a dramatic

vertical. Making as it does a structure that is bold and never changing, regardless of the season, meant that this yew was of fundamental importance to the look of the composition. Since a tree like this will eventually make such a strong statement, I found it hard to get the balance right at first and, unsure of myself, kept moving it. Last year, fed up with shilly-shallying and feeling confident enough to assume the yew had undergone its final upheaval – and to avoid further temptation – I planted it with a rose, and forcibly twined the rose round the tree. Now the Irish yew is fixed forever: I cannot possibly be provoked into moving it to another site. In winter the black pillar stands unadorned, but in summer its cat's-tail is circled with a moss rose, *Rosa centifolia muscosa*, one of the 'roses of a hundred petals'. The mossy buds and stems are so irresistible to the touch that I never feel impatient for them to open. Unfortunately, it's likely to climb faster than the yew gains height; any day now I shall become a bully and inhibit its impulse.

Bullying in this garden is mandatory, and torture is in the ascendancy. When a friend who had known our previous garden visited this one, in dismay she confided to a mutual friend: 'What's happened to Mirabel? She's got problems.' (I feel that about chefs who cut strawberries in half.) 'The woman's gone mad!' Yes, probably. It depends which way you face. For me this garden had to be something different, I didn't want ghosts plaguing me with reminders; here I am working on discovery and detachment. Continually experimenting with different ideas, I'm trying to find out what succeeds and what doesn't while not becoming distraught over constant botches. After all, I don't need to compromise. The garden is mine, I'm solely responsible, and having no one with whom to share it means I can blunder here and there in the knowledge that next year I may have a change of heart affecting no one but my plants and myself.

Influenced by the French and their way with shears, which had so impressed me when I was visiting and writing about their gardens, I wanted to re-create that spirit of serenity they seem to achieve with such intuitive ease. They cut, snip, pare and whittle in pursuit of Gallic sobriety – something utterly at odds with our national pastime. With their plant-molesting in my sights, an over-vigorous *Rubus thibetanus* is about to be given the French treatment – or else it must be press-ganged to take root beside the compost where its ghostly stems can draw a veil over the works. Tyranny in the garden is an ongoing trait that I'm cultivating along with my plants. And unless you are a cautious gardener, which I'm not, it's essential in a limited space to assume autocracy as a way of life. Particularly here, as I have just planted my thirty-sixth tree since the first in 1991.

The longer I work in it, the more I think the outlines and shapes of the dominant plantings are what make this garden – if anything does. It's certainly not flowers. I hardly have any, except for those in pots or in little openings at the foot of the wall. Most of the flowers are those on the shrubs, the clematis and the climbing roses. But the outline of the eight pleached lime trees along the southern boundary, decapitated at twelve feet, already works well by creating the form and movement which I had imagined but had never thought could really happen. What a pity. Had I known, I would have had the confidence to plant another row at the same time, along the opposite side of the garden.

These eight were planted in a hurry – which was unfortunate, because tree-planting is a favourite undertaking, and anyway trees deserve time spent on them – but dusk was falling rapidly at three-thirty on a November afternoon and it was dark by the time the last one went in. As we stamped each sapling down I became more and more excited. I'd wanted these trees for weeks, but the nurseryman kept postponing the day he would bring them. Later, when the job was done and the trees had been in for barely three hours, I was already aware of their presence. I can't explain it, but there they were, flimsy, yet so fundamental to the place that their brief existence already changed the personality of the garden. I couldn't see them, but the installation of eight tall strangers just there, outside, kept me restless, continually being drawn to the window to peer into the darkness and send the trees waves of felicity. I was their captive from that moment.

As the limes grew I tied canes to the two rows of fledgling branches and cut back all other side shoots. After four years I was able to remove the canes and tie one extended branch to the next, so that now they are intertwined like two lines of dancers in a *taverna*. To be able to see sunlight through their fluttering leaves – which is how I visualized the effect long before I'd decided on which trees they would be – it's necessary to cut their foliage to the minimum. Yet every spring I get even more pleasure from the trees in bud, the slender red twigs with crimson bracts the shape of finger-nails from which the nascent leaves develop in alternate folds. I hate 'rubbing out' the incipient buds on the trunk, but it has to be done if a lightweight structure is to be maintained. Without the canes, and quite by chance, the trees have grown into wavy green billows against the sky. A few people have remarked on it, saying how clever to have this undulating outline; but it isn't – it's just another of those fortunate happenings, which came about because I couldn't balance on the top of the steps and reach high enough to force the branches together more rigidly.

The twelve eucalyptus flanking the path – which I persecuted with the idea of creating pairs of silvery-grey globes no higher than four feet, marching towards the steps – have been a wash-out. They now work as a fault line running the length of the path – my fault. When I rang the specialist nursery in Wales to order the trees, I told the man what I intended doing with them. He told me he'd never heard of anyone cutting eucalyptus in that way. (For good reason, as it turned out.) But I don't regret my folly a bit; I don't want security as the plinth from which to garden, I want imagination and inconsequence; sophistry and guesswork. Knowing where you're going in the gardening world can sometimes be an awful let-down, as I've gathered from talking to those who've been doing it for years, and still they wring their hands over their own misplaced plantings.

So much for my experiment with the eucalyptus: if the trees didn't succumb to my butchery, the frost killed half of them. The ones left are pinkish, pretty, and mark the path like pointless aberrations. I shall give them their heads for a bit, and perhaps trepan them next year. This indecision is an aspect of gardening I particularly like; I like the freedom – having failed in my attempt to browbeat the eucalyptus into one way of life, I admit defeat. It's now up to them; if a pair looks as though it might make an arch across the path, I may do that; on the other hand, if a little urchin haircut would be in keeping, that's what I shall do. But I'll not make up my mind until I've stood about pondering this summer – or perhaps next.

A quince I shaped into a goblet by tying it to canes and tightening the twine little by little, as I used to do when putting a new string on my violin, gave me such pangs of remorse each time I walked past it that last summer I relented and released its branches. At the beginning I'd imagined how one day quince flowers, fragile as porcelain, would form a decorative shape far removed from their tangled habit in the wild. Now, as I write, I see that the tree has myriads of flower buds, more than ever before. Coming late, as they do, is an advantage as far as late frosts are concerned. Yet unless summer lingers long, the quinces have barely time enough to ripen into heavy yellow fruits, so hard to cut but worth the struggle for the fragrant smell when they're cooking, a scent that insinuates its way into every crevice in the house. And although my intention had been to give the quince its freedom – like releasing Chinese feet from bondage – the tree so far has kept its enforced shape, while breaking into leaf along previously naked branches. (I must control the temptation to anthropomorphize when writing of things like this. I feel a warm compatibility with the tree that is likely to leach into words – asinine and mawkish.)

Every town garden should have a fruit tree, whether cherry, plum, peach or mulberry. As I desperately wanted

one reminder of country orchards among all this muti-
lation, I planted a Bramley apple. The tree is left un-
chastened. It already leans, so that in years to come
I imagine with what pleasure someone will admire its
unregimented outline amid the rectangular back gardens
that surround us. But the mistake I've made with this
young tree is not to have curtailed its fecundity last year.
This is the second year I've left a massive crop of apples on
without appreciating that the tree is still adolescent. The
thin boughs drooped under the weight of fruit, until by July
five forked poles were needed to prop them up. Belatedly
in August I came to my senses and picked the whole crop,
which amounted to two basketfuls of uselessly unripe fruit.
I know now I should never have left the apples on the tree
in the first place. But it was always Michael who tended our
fruit trees in the other garden. I'm learning, I'm learning
– through empiricism not expertise.

Besides the Bramley, I have no intention either of
bludgeoning an amelanchier, a *Prunus* 'Autumnalis' and
two different acers that I've planted, but a pair of columnar
apple trees have to be regularly trimmed to maintain their
shape and a pair of Irish yews are kept clipped and corseted
with wire to make architectural pillars either side of the
steps. A couple of ordinary 'Kilmarnock' willows, whose
natural deportment is to weep copiously, have been cut
with flat bases and formal domed heads. This I did the
moment I brought them home from the market. They
are ruthlessly bobbed all through the summer, though
I actually like them better on days in winter when their
branches appear as misshapen rigging outlined in frost.
No one who visits the garden recognizes the trees – which

is not surprising, considering that God intended them to have a pendulous habit. I wonder for how long they'll put up with this bullying. They've grown well; so tall, in fact, that I need a stepladder to maintain their smoothly domed heads. At their base I've planted lavender, never allowing it to flower but cutting it into static circles so that the trees appear to be rising from granite plinths. To those who are shocked by this treatment I hasten to say that elsewhere in the garden I have lots of lavender. And if I had never lopped it, I would never have experienced the recurring delight of cutting back into its young growth. My whole head, my hand, my arms and garments become infused. The scent is sharper, fresher than the weighty fragrance that comes in late summer when the plants have long been in flower, intoxicating the bees.

Thus are small rewards dotted about the garden: unexpected, heart-warming and sweet-smelling.

Last year a generous friend who has a town garden with few flowers but many rare and beautiful trees told me she had too many *Clerodendron trichotomum fargesii*, would I like one? Would I? I leapt at the offer. Never having seen it but always willing to put in one more tree (or 'large shrub', technically, but mine looks like a tree), I was delighted. When we planted the clerodendron it was already over twelve feet high. What a bizarre tree. Its white flowers and maroon calyces are complicated, too hard to appreciate at that height. So I brought a sprig into the house to scrutinize. The berries that follow are astonishing – bright blue, and more like the sort of earrings you'd find in a dressing-up box. I'm already mad about it, and hope that Anne is as pleased with the agapanthus I gave her in exchange. These particular plants have a personal history for me, one that goes back for more than a century.

They have been passed down through the same family for generations: I was given the agapanthus by an elderly lady who had had them from her mother and her great-aunt before then.

Nothing would tempt me to tinker with a eucryphia, a tree I love above all others in this garden. For years the jacaranda had been my aspiration among trees, unattainable and memorable. I had forever coveted that tree, even though I knew there wasn't a hope of growing one here. And then, one day, I saw a eucryphia.

You know how it is; you see something somewhere, and nothing consequently can eradicate that first impression, even though in the passing years your imaginative allegiance has perhaps magnified its splendour. It must be ten years since I first saw a eucryphia at Powis Castle in mid Wales. Michael and I had forsaken our coarsening midsummer shambles as the garden slumped into the raucous toughs of August. We needed cheering. The tree, growing on one of the superbly planted terraces, was of such towering nobility it created its own drama. Nothing had prepared us for this. We stood in disbelief at the sight of a narrow upright tree clad from top to bottom with flowers looking as brittle as bone china. Ivory white, each contained a thicket of stamens with terracotta anthers, appearing almost luminous against the dark foliage. And this was August, a month not renowned for the refinement of its flora.

We had to have one. Every account of the tree that we read only whetted our hunger to possess it. With the misplaced enthusiasm that besets ignorant gardeners, we felt sure a *Eucryphia* × *nymansensis*, planted in a sheltered corner, would work. We failed, of course. It succumbed the first winter. Every year frost annihilated our trees and shrubs with lethal finality – and yet how, as gardeners, do you learn your limitations until you've tried things out for yourselves? Sadly, neither eucryphias nor magnolias, the rose 'Cooper's Burmese' or rosemary were for us, though we tried, we really did.

Now, years later, I'm trying again. I've planted *Eucryphia glutinosa* against a warm wall of the garden. Protected by the shaggy disorder of a buddleja and other shrubby things, it's survived two winters. More than anything I long for the tree to assume its stately deportment, and if the buds withstand a late frost, a white cascade of flowers will one day upstage the parched shrubs and overblown climbers of high summer. In July I watch its small buds, as narrow as pistachio nuts, with the anxiety of a neurotic, noting an ominous browning at their tips. Lack of water? Is this infernal drought going to thwart its flowering? Will its buds really open next month to reveal flowers of pearly innocence? Or instead shall I have to rely on the flimsy transience of bindweed in flower – a colonist I omitted to oust earlier in the year – as compensation for the perishable grace of a eucryphia in full flight? As late summer is not the most exciting time of year, the loss of a eucryphia could be a calamity. So far mine has produced a few flowers; enough to hold out promises of fulfilment in the summers that lie ahead.

The one tree I haven't planted, but which we tried twice to grow in the country, is a magnolia. They work so well in a town surrounded by unadorned architecture. But when I discovered that outside this house on a patch of municipal grass there's a huge magnolia, I reduced my tree-planting list from thirty-seven to thirty-six. From the first floor I look into its branches, willing the buds to remain tightly furled for as long as possible. A warm March is fatal – there's sure to be a late frost and the flowers will be done for overnight; but if spring is delayed, then the slow maturing of pink buds opening into white flowers on the leafless boughs becomes a protracted consummation. This is the tree's climax; the moment when magnolias, of whatever kind, have reached their summit. Looking at the tree in early summer, you see that it's true. But then on a golden day in October, standing underneath, you notice that each bright yellow leaf is outlined with dark brown. What an equally splendid way of dying.

Unfortunately, magnolias have one flaw. At least, this one does. It's so climbable. Children are drawn to its smooth branches as involuntarily as the rats in Hamelin Town were drawn to the Pied Piper. A few years ago boys swinging on one of the boughs broke it off, leaving the tree lopsided. I brought some of the smaller branches in and kept them in water for weeks. Miraculously the husks fell off and slowly the flowers opened. The tree is more than seventy years old and the lower branches have become heavy, forcing the bark to wrinkle at their joints as the hide does on an elephant. Please let the deity of sylviculture cast a protective spell over the tree for another half-century.

The grand panjandrum in my eyes is without doubt the *Buddleja alternifolia.* I love it to bits, not because it's either

rare or flamboyant, nor does it have a penetratingly eso-
teric scent: I love it for its cascading growth and abundance
of flowers. When I creep underneath to pull up the bindweed that invades this neighbourhood with the tenacity of
an octopus, I'm surrounded by twigs so insignificant they
seem unrelated to the flouncy skirts of violet flowers on
the outside. Here I have planted cyclamen. The wonder
of these flowers! They appear overnight after a sprinkle of
rain in autumn, so demure and self-effacing I might easily
miss them if I didn't know where to look. They thrust up
through the chopped bark, which appears far too coarse to
be pushed aside by such frail stems. Each year the buddleja
shading them has grown larger – in height and diameter. I
prune it only after flowering, otherwise I let the tree go in
whatever direction suits its habit. Not only does it fill the
space in this garden with wands, it flows over the fence
into my neighbour's – who fortunately never complains. (I
wonder: suppose I were to shear a little off the branches all
at one height, what would the tree look like? Spectacular
or deformed? The latter, probably, so I won't.)

A *Ceanothus* 'Cascade' that I've grown as a tree has
copper and green Viridiflora 'Artist' tulips planted underneath. What a union of colour. The orange and blue
are perfection – or would be, if I hadn't mistimed their
flowering. Of course the tulips come up long before the
ceanothus blooms – only imagination still holds that idyllic
image intact. But as usual, other compensations rise to
the surface. One day, staring closely at the tulips, I was
fascinated to find that the aphids, with their instinct for
survival, were clustered only along the green spines on
the petals, not against the coppery part. From a distance

the pests were utterly camouflaged, a fact that would have escaped me if I hadn't been grovelling about at the foot of the 'tree'.

With not enough space for a reptilian wisteria trunk draped along a wall, I've forced mine into a standard tree, with an eye to it becoming a tasselled parasol to be seen from the house. To begin with I wasn't ruthless enough when denying it its natural tendency to twist, so the trunk, although bound to a stake, now bulges in the most inelegant way. I've tried to conceal this malformation by swathing it with the ruffled pink petals of that most obliging rose, the 'Comte de Chambord'. Tied to the trunk of the wisteria, the rose gracefully conceals the tree's curvature. What a rose! Small as it is, this Portland rose keeps on flowering. Even one bloom brought into the house and placed in a bottle on my work table fills the room with a scent so intense it's quite out of scale with the size of the bush itself.

There's one misconception that's been a bother from the first. People informed me, quite misleadingly, that the debris 'wouldn't amount to much' now that I had such a small garden. Don't be fooled. If you're making a town garden for the first time, think long and hard. By what route (possibly through the house) and by what method will you cart the stuff out of the garden, and in the meantime where will you stack it? This is fundamental; it's a dilemma to be considered with your first stirrings of design. Obviously autumn is the worst season for rubbish, but don't be lulled into thinking there'll just be a manageable amount the rest of the year. There won't. Dealing with it is an ongoing and beastly chore. Manhandling it into blue plastic bags supplied by the Council is not the most winning way of filling time, though it's practical when they are then collected along with the household rubbish.

Derek Jarman said that lawns are 'the enemy of a good garden'. That's strong stuff; but yes, they are overrated as the universal ingredient for *every* garden. It seems to be taken for granted that we should begin with a lawn, but after a year here I began to find the maintenance of the one I'd inherited a chore. The constant upkeep was an unnecessary burden which gave me no pleasure whatsoever. In its place I laid four inches of chopped bark which, whenever I want to plant a shrub, I scoop aside to dig a hole. The colour of the bark, which varies in tones from light mahogany to dark chocolate according to the weather, is good for making an unobtrusive background to plants. Slowly I've put in more and more trees, shrubs and spring bulbs, until no one notices the absence of a lawn. I would have paved the area, as I've seen done abroad, which makes for perfect harmony between structure and plants. But expense and lack of access pushed me in a certain direction, and if it is not ideal, it has the advantage of being easy to walk on whatever the time of year.

Undoubtedly the garden is child-unfriendly and growing more so every year, with an increasing number of pots, and with shrubs and trees taking up space. At the far end where steps lead to the door going nowhere there's a bench so concealed only my granddaughter Cassandra and I know where it is. Secretive, almost buried under the flowers and later the fruit of an ancient elderflower tree, is a wooden seat for two people seeking a clandestine rendezvous. Cassandra may not be able to throw a ball about in my garden, but here she can lurk unseen and be sure of remaining undiscovered.

Losing One's Head, or Loss of Face

Experiments are a continuing part of gardening. Whenever I think it's time to be sensible about the garden and to go for what does work, I'm goaded on by remembering a Danish scientist who invented a robotic bee to entice real bees to a source of nectar. Now there's madness. A similar lunacy, and only slightly more problematical perhaps – but it might work – would be to grow sempervivums along the roof ridge of the kitchen extension. An encrustation of roseate plants nesting amid rabbit netting fixed to the tiles would make a decorative spine to a rather boring roof. And why stop at houseleeks? Could I grow cyclamen? In autumn would they flutter like butterflies against the sky, or would it be too sunny up there? Or after a downpour, would the courtyard be strewn with their corpses?

My eucalyptus scheme turned out to be a flop, but I've already shrugged that one off. Experimenting in the kitchen is an acknowledged pastime; experimenting in the garden less so. Why? Are you more likely to look foolish? But if your heart is in it and you can remain laid-back, then many wild gardening ideas are worth pursuing, or at least giving a second thought.

In addition to my method of binding a yew with a rose, I've experimented with other things. By giving a spiraea the third-degree treatment after letting it flower for the last few years, I've turned the bush into a large ball so densely white in spring the leaves are concealed and a cobweb of scent smelling of honey surrounds the plant. The rose 'Tuscany Superb', which is far too big for where I have it, has to be mauled annually as I tie the branches round and round on themselves to make a compact shape. Subjecting the bush to this restraint has resulted in buds breaking out along every horizontal twig, so that by July the rose is covered with dark crimson flowers.

On the counter of the town's delicatessen stand cylinders of cheese that when uncut look like weathered rocks. The illusion of pumice, verdigris and strata of calcification appeared so real I wanted to carry one home to stand at the top of my garden steps; instead I compromised. The owners of the shop saved me the best bits of cloth from the larger cheeses, which I cut and glued onto plastic flower pots. I imagined how their appearance would be a pleasing alternative to over-shrill terracotta, and how the rumpled folds of mottled and moulded material would give the courtyard the splendour of limestone antiquity. Unfortunately, I hadn't foreseen that such pungent material would prove an elixir to woodlice and ants; by the end of the winter I found the bottom of the cloth devoured. But alchemy is fun; and as an alternative to spinning flax into gold, turning plastic pots into rock is irresistible. So I shall try again and this time, to discourage predator insects, use something to counteract the reek of cheese.

There are definite times of the year when the garden moves into my own personal space – not physically, but it encroaches on my thoughts and puts an end to conjectures and wild surmises. This is the moment to jettison every frivolous thought, take up my pen and fill in a bulb order. Unfortunately, in my first year here I ran into problems. I'm hopelessly innumerate, and now that they've left off putting the comma in the figure one thousand, I get moithered by noughts. How many are there? Is that ten thousand, or a million? Having filled in my bulb order and laboriously added up the total, checking and rechecking until I came up with the same number several times, I was finally defeated by seeing there was a space left for VAT. Value Added Tax at 17½ per cent. I ask you! What an enigma. Even with a gadget I couldn't work it out, because I couldn't work the gadget. Which way should the decimal point go? Am I working from left to right, or right to left? It was dusk and the shops were shut, otherwise I might have asked Phyllis at the delicatessen to do the sum. (Loss of face, at my age, is immaterial.) Instead I tore up the order, and the following spring had no new bulbs in the garden. However, it all ended happily because I now have the sense to look first to see if the tax is included in the price. If it isn't, I turn to another bulb supplier.

Lying in the bath or waiting on a station platform, making mayonnaise or with a mind glazing over while someone relates the complete story of a film – all are good times to conceive giddy plans or high-falutin notions, however improbable. Back gardens, in contrast to pastoral ones, are just begging to be taken over.

The Splendour of Vegetables

Kitchen gardens can be so beautiful they should be elevated in the gardening hierarchy to the equal of rose enclosures. I know nothing about growing vegetables, but their appearance either in the ground or on the plate is a constant enjoyment.

The pleasure of pushing open a wicket gate and moving about a well-tended vegetable garden is something no amount of exotic vegetables on supermarket shelves can replace. Gourmets may bless the vast variety of produce to be had nowadays in shops, but walking down those over-lit aisles is far removed from walking through an old-fashioned kitchen garden. Regimented rows lined up with exactitude are restful on the eye. They exemplify control; an ordered world; someone's enviable obsession with precision and the culmination of patient attention. The result for the rest of us is the pleasurable anticipation of a dish of fresh peas.

Going beyond mere hedonistic feasting as a motivation for what to grow in a kitchen garden – there is the visual effect, which can overwhelm both the expert and the ignoramus with its purity of formation. Onions, which propel themselves out of the ground until they are sitting on the earth, catch the light on their globular skins. The foliage of asparagus is flimsy, the filigree seed-heads of leeks are worth bringing in from the rain; purple-sprouting broccoli carries ruffs of frilly leaves; courgette and runner bean flowers are bright, and the rosy shoulders of radishes rise with startling rapidity. Continental parsley or our native mossy sort, chives and thymes, all fill a corner of the garden with their varying habits and density of green. Silvery artichokes, a relative of those other magnificent natives of the Mediterranean, the cardoons, are too handsome to ignore, with their classically shaped leaves similar to the acanthus. Fennel, fleshy purslane and a whole tribe of salads, such as oak-leaved and lamb's lettuce (*mâche*), take up vinaigrette dressing and are good to eat before native salads are available.

As for the other senses, there is the unforgettable smell when for the first time in your life you pick a tomato; the intimate rasp made by the dead leaves of corn-on-the-cob before the stems are felled; or the sinuous growth of yellow, orange and coral pumpkins and gourds with their warts, ribs, mottling and bulbous shapes seen amid their barbaric foliage.

Perhaps having pride in a vegetable you've grown is more understandable than similar feelings for a flower or shrub? What satisfaction, laced with complacency, when you harvest a basketful of young carrots, French beans, asparagus or infant courgettes with unblemished trumpets – golden flowers that when fresh are good to eat – that you've raised yourself. Liquid manure in a peach is quite a thought, but so is the contemplation of the coffee grounds, orange peelings, household sweepings and moulted dogs' hair that may have gone into a crop of potatoes. Then each potato, lying on the plate, is an exquisite culinary experience far too good to be desecrated by gravy.

The first time I saw vegetables growing among flowers was on the continent. Under the balcony hung with scarlet geraniums of a châlet in Austria were cabbages and leeks interspersed with yellow daisies. Outside village houses in France, kitchen gardens are planted with arbitrary crops of flowers and vegetables growing amid a few fruit trees. The method may appear feckless, but I was told that as long as more compost is given to the vegetables than to the flowers, the system works.

In the Balkans, where people may have to walk or ride their donkeys for several miles outside the villages to cultivate their plots, you may see a few zinnias growing among the aubergines, peppers, courgettes and beans. Roses and vines twine over a frame sheltering a well surrounded by pots of basil and geraniums, giving the place a negligent charm that would be inept if consciously attempted in our gardens.

Reading about American vegetable gardens, I learned a lot about the Midwest. According to Jane Anne Staw and Mary Swander in their book *Parsnips In The Snow*, they met a man in Galesburg, Illinois, famous locally for his okra, who told them: 'I just took my seeds and throwed them out. Didn't think it was gonna do nothing. But it come up and just growed wild.' A professor at Iowa University abhorred such heedless planting. He planned that his purple beets should harmonize with red onions, and when his design of green and crimson lettuces was ready they had to be harvested alternately to maintain the pattern.

Potagers have caught on in Britain in a big way, but inevitably our inherited walled kitchen gardens, with their dimensions on such a scale that they need a squad of gardeners to tend them, are literally going to the wall. These reminders of a time when country houses were supplied with a boundless quantity of fresh fruit and vegetables are becoming rare. Circumstances have meant that the one remaining gardener can only cultivate a small proportion of the land. Against the four high walls skeletons of once productive espaliered fruit trees remain upright, kept there by the same iron nails that first forced them into position. Yet they are worth visiting still for the beauty of their decaying decrepitude.

Flowers versus vegetables. If you had only a small garden, which would come first? Aesthetics or appetite? Alas, answers are never that simple.

Pots and Urns

Pots are among the most important features in this garden. They are objects that work at the other end of garden design: their presence can be as germane as trees, but with the advantage that they can be moved. They can clutter a bare corner at one time of year and then be re-sited to stand beside my bench when flowers and scents are at their best. But pots are hell to water. Every summer I swear to cut down on their number, yet their versatility is so tempting I do exactly the opposite. I acquire more, even though I'm not actually much good at pot gardening. No, that's an understatement; most of the time I'm hopeless. When I see what other people do, I have to face the reality that my moments of triumph are few. The pots are as ungainly as my flower arranging – but long ago I solved that by putting a single flower into a wine bottle, a method that requires no skill. A whole lot of bottles pushed together make a group of varying height and of variously coloured glass, according to what we have been drinking lately. When I do this with a single rose in each bottle on the window still, the effect of seeing each one against the light is very different from the way roses appear in the garden, or the way they look in a Dutch painting of a vase of flowers, where every pleat and fray on a petal is painstakingly delineated and insects among the blooms are biologically accurate.

Some of the things I plant in the pots thrive – but lots don't, so in the end I have learnt not to be adventurous and to stick to things that do work well for me. The little alpine phloxes, which begin to look promising early in April when they produce a foggy-pink haze belying the colour to come, are fool-proof. Without fail each May they make hummocks so densely covered with baby-blue flowers that they look like plump footstools either side of the steps. Sometimes a pot of them stands next to frilly pink tulips, suggesting naff bedrooms; at other times one stands beside a yellow café chair, because to me yellow and blue (or orange and blue) is perhaps the supreme colour combination. As I never change the soil because the pots have narrow necks, I rely on feeding them well. But I don't take their annual fidelity for granted. Each spring I expect it to be their last.

Ordinary pansies (the blue, blue ones, not the more indigo kind), petunias, forget-me-nots and yellow violas all drift and sprawl together as colours on a palette. Campanulas redeem the fierce and relentless red of English terracotta pots that take years to weather. I've knocked out the bottoms of some and planted lavenders, hoping they'll root down into the ground vigorously enough to make bushy heads to hide those roses with skeletal frames. If my plan works, these pots are not for moving: their unglazed clay will formalize the lavender surrounding the roses 'Golden Wings' or the thorny stems of 'William Lobb'. When I run out of ideas for what to plant in these aggressively-coloured pots, I paint them using a water-based paint that soaks into the clay and forms a translucent coloured skin much more subtle in tone than painting them with the proper stuff gives. The method is practical, too; next year I can paint them other colours according to what I'm going to plant.

But by far the most successful of my pots are those that I leave empty. Crowded together, they look as though I know what I'm doing and am about to fill them. Actually I'm not. I keep them empty because I like the sense of optimism they give about the place. This summer there are nineteen in the garden. Some are solitary, some are in small groups; they look full of potential but I won't have to face the reality of disillusionment when what I plant dies. (No watering, either.) They appear to be on the way, but they need never arrive.

Larger three-foot urns stand empty too. Shrubs lean against them, roses flop over them, and at their feet small plants snuggle down cosily. Various two-handled pitchers mark the entrance to the path; others are unadorned Greek flower pots made by hand. The potters' thumb

marks turn them into intimate objects rather than manufactured duplications. Their outlines may be wonky but
the colour is that of barely cooked shortbread, or certain
Labrador dogs. Unplanted, they stand as a family on a
slate shelf put up specially to hold them, making their
own shadows one against the other. Slate and milky clay
are gentle to the eye.

A few years ago I visited Jim Keeling's Whichford Pottery
in Warwickshire, where he employs about twenty local
people. None were potters before he took them on, but
they have each had the chance to work at all the processes
involved in making Ali Baba jars, scalloped, lily, barrel or
basket pots and troughs. Downstairs are two kilns and the
'blunger' where the clay is mixed, and upstairs the 'throwing' takes place – a process with a touch of prestidigitation
about it, it looks so easy. Instead of a foot-propelled wheel,
it's powered by electricity. The transformation of a lump
of clay into a work of art has the same magic that you feel
when watching a wood-carver at work. Each potter puts his
or her initials on the piece before the upended pots are left
to slightly dry out before being decorated with anything
from classical festoons and garlands to running patterns,
medallions or geometric motifs. Finally they're fired, and
it's then that the colour and frost-proofing is achieved.

Periodically Keeling has a sale of 'seconds', but don't
only visit for that reason, go for the pleasure of seeing
craftsmen turning earth into artefacts.

Apertures

'Apertures'. That's a word to carry in your pocket as you contemplate moving to a new garden. It has a certain provocation to it that opens vistas in the mind as well as signifying views from a garden onto landscape. Few things are more brilliant than finding an arch or a window framing something beyond. But if you have a panoramic view, how even more imperative it is to frame it. If a view isn't hidden, you're condemned to live with something far too indigestible. A panorama overwhelms a garden; it devours the foreground; it leans over you, and your flowers, and irrevocably destroys intimacy. Can anyone forget their first visit to Hidcote, and the stunning revelation, at the end of the avenue of pleached hornbeams on stilts, of that unexpected expanse of landscape: the Vale of Evesham, spread beyond a foreground field of grazing sheep?

In the summer I visited a garden where, across from the house and a paved courtyard with flowers in the cracks, several steps led up to a gap in the hedge. Tall and dark, the hedge enclosed the courtyard like a room. Carefully placed to be seen from indoors, a narrow opening had been cut in the yew framing meadows, oak trees and the blue distance of agricultural England. Without the hedge, the landscape would have trespassed on the garden.

C. Alexander, in his book *A Pattern of Language*, writes of a Japanese Buddhist monk living on a mountain: 'On the far side of the courtyard there was a slit in the wall, narrow and diagonal . . . As a person walked across the court . . . for an instant, he could see the ocean.' Alexander goes on to say that the more open a view is, the more it shouts, 'and the intensity of its beauty will no longer be accessible to the people who live there'.

In Greece we let the holm oaks hide our view of the Ionian Sea except for deliberate openings where at sunset the lights of the fishing boats could be seen passing to and fro in 'lavender water tinged with pink'. But whether you have a view onto the sea or across a vast landscape, hide it. Alexander's wisdom is nowhere more valid than in a garden. Even here, which isn't exactly an elevated site, I can contrive a 'window'. By cutting a hole in the branches of a hazel and a holly tree at the end of the garden, I've let in a piece of horizon, part sky and part woods and hills on the margins of the town: the garden has a breathing hole. When I walk the length of the path I feel the magnetism of distance, when everywhere else there are frontiers. The aperture has to be re-cut every spring, after the foliage has returned and it's possible to see what bits need trimming. The pruning isn't anything important, and I do it rather haphazardly because the branches that need trimming are almost out of reach. But every time it's worth the effort; it's rather like releasing built-up pressure from the garden.

Buildings and Benches

The ugly garden shed that was here when I moved in was
far too practical to jettison. I turned it round so that I
can't see the sloping glass side – intended for sunlight
and dedicated propagators – and the end with the door
in it now faces the garden. The shed is painted the same
eucalyptus-leaf colour as the trellis that runs along on top
of the boundary walls and fence. The only way I could get
the precise shade I wanted was to take a leaf of young
eucalyptus to the paint shop. There are those who, like
musicians with perfect pitch, can carry a colour faultlessly
in their mind's eye. I'm never that confident; when I am
and think I recognize a particular tone, whether of a rose,
fabric or paint, I'm invariably out by a minor variation that
can be crucial to the result.

A thatch of *Clematis montana* now completely hides the
ungainly outline of the shed. When this is in flower the
grey-green of the building and the pink of the flowers
are so sickly together that they could be the setting for
a third-rate operetta. A few months ago the edifice was
radically transformed into a work of art when Jessie Jones,
a student at the St Martin's School of Art, painted a
trompe-l'oeil on the door. I wanted a window looking into
a potting shed with a barn owl on the sill looking out.
What she has done is brilliant; seed trays, skeins of raffia,
worn gloves, tools and earthenware pots are deceptively

real behind a lifesize barn owl standing on the window ledge and gazing out with baleful intent as though on the look-out for mice. What fun to turn something as prosaic as an ugly pre-constructed garden shed into a theatrical production. When the clematis is in flower, sprawling and effervescing above the *trompe-l'oeil*, its tendrils frame the painting as well as clambering along the branches of the pleached limes. The whole effect is of something way out of my control. It is. I look up at the clematis after it's flowered and feel I ought to be doing something about it – but what? The question hangs in the air unanswered and I've done nothing yet. If the roof caves in, I'll have to – meanwhile, I feel well content with the whole affair.

Last year my daughters gave me a long wooden bench with arms. Originating in Hungary, it must have stood in some elegant country loggia for years, judging from the dusty-blue paint softened through decades of ageing. On the inside of the lid of the storage space beneath the seat is a tattered poster showing the Austro-Hungarian Imperial family with Kaiser Franz-Josef and the Kaiserin Elisabeth surrounded by their children. Whose hands were they that bothered to stick the poster under the lid many years ago? And why there? Whoever they were, they would be amused – or perhaps saddened – to know that the bench has travelled such a long way from its origins, to end its life in an English garden. I get almost as much pleasure wondering about its past as I do from sitting on its seat.

All through its first summer the presence of the bench at the far end of the garden changed my attitude to this area, which up until then had been the place for compost, the wheelbarrow, bricks, surplus stones and broken pottery, and for bonfires. But when autumn came I was faced with the problem of what I should do with such a large piece of furniture made from soft wood never intended to winter outside. Some people advised me to make a fitted plastic cover for it, others suggested that I should paint it with a colourless protective varnish; in the end we struggled to carry it into the hall, but none of these possibilities was the ultimate solution. Yet gardens have a way of coercing you into undertaking things you never intended doing, and when you have, you wonder why you waited so long.

What was needed, of course, was a weatherproof shell, in the form of a building – a building of grace that would fit into the garden and be as handsome as the bench itself, its construction as decorative as the garden shed. But who could make such a thing? Of course. With confidence I asked Richard Craven, the man who'd made the tree platform in our country garden and, more recently, the cleft-oak archway in this garden. He understands wood, grain and stone, has imagination and an instinctive eye for proportions: I knew we'd work together harmoniously. At first we might be carried away by schemes for fabulous pavilions, but I knew in the end, when we'd sobered down, Richard would come up with exactly the right design. What was needed against the long brick wall was a building that sat down robustly, rather than something that floated.

The dimensions enclose the bench without crowding it. From this point – facing south and standing on a slightly raised foundation – the distant woods can be seen beyond the branches of the pleached limes. The floor is constructed from large oyster- and apricot-coloured Indian tiles, the roof is curved and made of copper, which is already corroding into the distressed turquoise of pieces of coarse jewellery I have from Nepal.

On the inside, curved slats with gaps between reveal an arched blue ceiling. The slats are pale apricot and the boards of the sides are painted alternately a greyish purple and coral, to give the feel of being in a striped pavilion. The whole of the three-sided building is made of chestnut and because, although the grain is wonderful, I didn't want it to look too rustic in such an unrustic setting, the outside is painted with a watery wash of lettuce green and greyish purple so thin it allows the grain of the wood to show through.

Misleadingly, the building has become known as the Cat House – not from any nefarious Texan connections, but because from the moment it was finished my neighbours' cats took shelter there. In the rain, muddy paw marks gave them away, in winter I saw their prints in the snow, leading to and from the shelter. The Cat House is beautiful.

A bench with its own carapace is a great persuader. Before I had it I could safely walk to the end of the garden with my mind intent on the job in hand. Not any longer. Passing the place without going in is almost impossible, especially as I leave cushions lying about on the bench so that even alone I'm waylaid. When a gale is buffeting the garden I pause here to draw breath, relishing the comfort of being momentarily out of the elements. Passing by, I used to brush aside spiders' webs clinging to the eaves – until one day, staring vacantly out from the inside, I had time to see that the gold spiders like the house as much as the cats do. They make their webs not only under the eaves but spanning the bars either side of the entrance. The webs are so perfect, caught in the moist light of autumn and trembling slightly as the spiders work them, that now I take them as part of the building, an added decoration I shall no longer brush aside with housewifely pernicketiness.

Having the Cat House in the part of the garden until recently used for the practical mechanics of gardening has meant an upheaval. The area now has to be taken seriously. I cannot indulge my somewhat laid-back approach and leave things as they were. Bonfires will be banished from the magnificent stone circle my son-in-law made to ensure that, in a dry spell, the bark chippings didn't catch and set the whole garden into one dramatic conflagration, which would have justifiably vexed the neighbours and – worse – scattered the cats. So Zenon's 'threshing floor' has changed from a totally functional place to one for frivolous embroidery: I'm planting different ornamental ivies to corkscrew round the edges in a border of pinkish chippings. If the whole thing sounds too itsy-witsy, it well may be. This is the first year I've tried it. Should the pink gravel (it only really looks pink when it rains) appear out-of-place, I can easily scuff bark over to conceal it and try another colour or another material.

Ivies

After years, I've just about come to terms with ivies. I can at last feel my temperature rising, but it's taken a long time. I don't think I ever would have managed it if it hadn't been for Jane Fearnley-Whittingstall's comprehensive book on the subject and a supportive gardening friend, Katherine Swift, who insisted that I should be less biased and look slowly through a catalogue she lent me. As a result of the enthusiasm of these two women, I now have ivies in my garden – although I still think they are the sort of plants that entirely depend for their effectiveness on where and how they're grown. Unlike fennel or euphorbias and, particularly, ferns, which each have an intrinsic beauty and would look good growing even on a fire escape, ivies demand a careful consideration of where to place them.

I do like the way one thing leads to another. My daughters gave me a bench for my birthday; that produced the Cat House to shelter it; the Cat House meant I couldn't sit there facing bonfires, so in place of bonfires I'm embroidering with different ivies; and this quite naturally led on to the question of what to put in the centre of the 'threshing floor'. Without realizing that I was searching for ideas, subconsciously I was receptive to any solution that rose to the surface. When I saw an advertisement in *Gardens Illustrated* for drystone urns, I knew that was what I'd been looking for. I rang the number in Scotland immediately.

Joe Smith of Dumfries, who's also made a number of sculptures in the Forest of Grizedale in Cumbria, makes the urns in three sizes, using whichever of three kinds of slate you prefer. Mine is made from Lake District slate the colour of rue, and it's his smallest size, about three feet high with a three-foot girth. But it has only a seven-inch diameter base, which gives a surprising elegance to something so substantial and rotund. Utterly symmetrical, the urn is a work of art. The thin layers of slate, one overlapping the other, make their own shadows. In rain, it turns into a prehistoric creature, perhaps a species of palaeolithic crustacean. In the right, important setting, how splendid a pair of Joe's five-foot-high urns would look.

Mirrors

At idle moments the best ideas emerge. Sitting on the bench inside the Cat House not long after it was finished with a mind lying fallow while I contemplated the limes and the chestnut fence behind them, I thought of mirrors. Once the thought had germinated, how easy to move into overdrive. But how was I to try this out before committing myself to having one cut? Tamsin and I took it in turns to hold the bathroom mirror at various angles and levels to see if and how it might work. The more we fiddled about, reflecting this and that, the more I became convinced.

Unlike trees, instant effects like this one are easily achieved. A large piece of looking-glass is now in place, standing about five inches above the ground and entirely filling one long panel of the fence. Slightly tilted to avoid seeing an image of oneself from across the garden, the mirror reflects the foreground of the drystone urn, the yew tied up by a rose, and a collection of pots. Tendrils of roses and clematis surround it, the glass reflecting the reverse sides of those bits that hang across it. Of course, no one stops at one mirror. Having seen what it did to the garden, and urged on by a friend, I've put in another three, increasing certain plants by fifty per cent and giving an illusion of open-handed hospitality in doubling the number of painted chairs around the table.

Reaction to the mirrors varies. Walking along the path, some visitors pass by and then do a double take; others are momentarily fooled into thinking the ground flows into further gardens. A few Crouchers are so intent on plants they leave the garden without having noticed there were any mirrors at all, and the cats wisely knew from the first it was a bit of jiggery-pokery. They aren't idiots. I had been concerned for the birds, but because the mirrors are at ground level they don't fly into them, as they occasionally do into window panes. And some people instantly give themselves away by solemnly asking me, 'But how do you keep the mirrors clean?' Keep them clean? Good God, I've never thought about it! It wouldn't ever occur to me until, and if, it becomes necessary, and even then I can't count on myself to bother.

Rust

Rust brings the perfect colour into a garden – and I'm not talking about that common disease on hollyhocks which makes their leaves appear as foxed as some of my engravings that are badly in need of reframing. I'm talking of rust on metal. I never use anti-corrosive; anything that will go rusty I leave untreated, almost everything else I paint. Not just some of the flower pots but white café chairs are now the blue of delphiniums, others the same sea-grey-green as the shed, trellis and other things about the place. The combination of these two normally incompatible colours has an oddly calming quality, and their tones work particularly well with roses or deep crimson clematis.

On the brick wall of the extension in the courtyard that I had painted ochre the year I arrived, there is now a piece of furniture around which honeysuckle and clematis circle in a gold and white tangle. Zenon made it. All I wanted was a couple of roughly-built shelves of packing-case wood, although it's hard for anyone as skilful as Zenon to produce a genuine botched job. Like most craftsmen, he has too much pride. (I suppose if I were a knitter I might demur at being asked to deliberately drop stitches.) The 'book shelf', unsanded and knocked together with nails, has a scalloped roof and gaps between the boards on which to stand chipped slipware dishes, bits of cracked painted pottery, and any faded coloured objects I haven't had the heart to throw out. There are also relics I've dug up in the garden, such as broken crockery and rusty hinges; and sometimes a pretty pot of something so delicate and chaste it needs to be seen only at eye level: an auricula, a sinisterly open-throated orchid, or a snake's-head fritillary. As soon as the shelves were finished and I'd painted the whole thing with a thin wash of green paint, a blackbird nested there. She found the worn-looking roofed shelves, contrived as they were, a cosier place to bring up young than the ceanothus on the opposite wall where the cat lingered with ominous intent.

Unreasonable Behaviour

How often in the arena of gardening do I come up against the stone wall of reason! I don't like it. I don't want to be reasonable; there's time for that in the grave. What I want is adventure, innovation, foolishness and discovery. Now, entirely thanks to reason, I've learnt to be devious in the paint shop.

Through experience, I've learnt to ignore the advice of technicians. Whenever the shopkeeper asks me what I want paint for, I lie. I tell him it's for sitting-room walls. When I did tell the truth, that it was for outside – for window frames, for doors, garden sheds, the trellis; for iron chairs and terracotta pots – the man threw up his hands in horror. 'Outside? You must use GLOSS.' But that was just the paint I did not want. I was after matt paint, something with a bloom to it, paint that breathed, paint that revealed rather than appearing opaque. Occasionally gloss is useful, when there's a need for the contrast of a band of shiny paint to highlight the rim of a pot, but otherwise I'd ask him to mix small amounts of emulsion.

Once, in an effort to achieve just the roan colour I wanted for an Ironbridge 'fern' garden seat, I tried using packets of dye from Woolworth combined with a fixative. Another time I rubbed blue-black ink into raw wood to get the shadowy effect I needed. The pollen from the stamens of lilies adheres to my hand so tenaciously, and the golden colour is so bold that I'm going to try doing something with that. Curry paste might work, but unfortunately it's not the same as pollen, neither the colour, the texture or the smell. For a gritty texture I did once try crushing duck-egg shells into a coarse powder – the colour was lovely, but I could never find the right adhesive base. Shoe polish, strong black coffee, beetroot water and mustard powder have all come in handy for certain things – otherwise it's emulsion and other water-based paints any professional would repudiate for the uses I put them to.

Textile designers know all about this, working as they so often do with natural dyes, but gardeners are never fired-up to experiment with pigments. Yet you can muck about endlessly trying this or that combination. The fact that the colour fades after a few years is an advantage – teenagers go mad to achieve that look with their jeans – and without waiting years I long to produce the faded tone seen on shutters and wine-press doors in Italy, where summers of sun-baked weathering have crackled the paint to powder.

The texture of subdued paint used throughout a garden immediately gives the place an illusion of maturity, even if it's newly made. And if the paint isn't going to last for years, nor am I (though in a chemist's shop I was once handed a sample of 'Time Defying Foundation' that rather wimpishly I've never put to the test). People are too timid, too over-awed by the prescribed norm, whether it's the way you plant things or mix paints. I came up against this years ago when I used to buy upholstery material or curtain remnants with which to make clothes – the textures were far more exciting than stuff bought from the dressmaking department. But again I learned I should keep my mouth shut unless I wanted to be told that I couldn't use this or that fabric when making a jacket, waistcoat or skirt. 'Madam, it's meant for a sofa!' And once, because I don't have a loom but wanted to make my own material, I knitted it instead. The only knitting I can do is to-and-fro in plain stitch. When I was buying the wool in the shop here and was asked what I was going to make, I lied, naturally. Every knitting buff had already told me that one can't just make a large piece of knitting and then cut it up to make a jacket. But you can. If you're like me and can't follow patterns or knit anything but plain, let me reassure you that my method worked. Because I used a mixture of yarns including four-ply, knobbly, chenille, mohair, cotton and angora, when I cut out the jacket none of the threads unravelled. It even has inset pockets.

So where paint is concerned, forget reason. Ignore the professionals and mess with colours until you get the dusky plum or underside-of-mushroom tone on wood, earthenware or metal that you are wanting. I try out colours on pieces of wood, and all the surplus paint is spread over the walls of the downstairs lavatory, until now the room looks like someone else's migraine.

Coming to Terms with My Limitations

'A gardener learns to play the hand he's been dealt,' wrote Michael Pollan in *Second Nature*. Fine. But before he has learnt, for how long does he lurch about packing the boot of the car with improbable temptations that are entirely wrong for his particular garden? In my case, far too long. The list of failures would be boring to relate. I only know that huge wall plants generously efflorescent, pools of meconopsis with the intensity of lapis, and dusty auriculas for which I craved with unappeased frustration kept me in a state of yearning resulting in misplaced confidence. Only slowly have I yielded; I am not rapacious now that I know more, and as I'm not a plantswoman a good many of the things in the garden come either from the market – where four times a week I can find most of the things I want – or else from some nearby nursery.

In other words, I'm playing the hand I've been dealt. I've learnt to use what surrounds me: pansies, those the curious colour of gangrenous meat; velvet-textured crimson petunias and others the pink of cherubs' bottoms; one or two shocking bedding plants abrasive enough to appease the lust of any Swiss municipal gardener; and numerous clematis and roses. But when there are uprooted clumps of snowdrops in the market, I do wince. They look so vulnerable, torn from the earth while they are still flowering; and although this is the way to transplant them, they remind me of puppies taken from their mother before they're properly weaned.

No one should be fooled into buying plants in flower, tempting us with the wizardry of instant gardening. The salesmanship is clever, but a con. And sometimes good things happen, as when a rose bought as anonymous-looking sticks turns out to be incorrectly labelled but more beautiful than the one I had intended to buy.

As I don't have the heart to remove them, several successful mishaps are now firmly established. Poppies, the kind so fiercely scarlet you feel like admonishing them with 'Temper! Temper!', have leaked all over the garden but are allowed to remain in their disparate array under the apple tree. Cassandra looks forward to the annual conflagration of scarlet when we gather the fallen petals for her to arrange in patterns. Too soon she'll grow to be more sophisticated, and then I'll be able to control them and try for subtle-coloured ones; in the meantime I put up with the cross-fertilization that annually reduces the garden to the colour of a field in Flanders.

Surrender

Roses. I didn't mean to do it. I really intended to practise self-restraint and grow only a few: this garden is small compared to the one where we allowed roses to grow to the bulk of elephants. But my resolution didn't last: the good nature of roses and their versatility demands more strength of character than I possess. Their scent alone is enough to make you lose your head. I never even put up a fight.

Rosa turkestanica, 'Comte de Chambord', 'Belle de Crécy', and others listed as small are fine, but what I like about gardening is that it makes a mockery of intentions. The result is that in no time I'm back to floral persecution.

'Blushing Lucy' is a Wichuraiana with predatory tendencies that belie her modest name. Her trusses of flowers, blooming later than the others, make over-exuberant
flounces of pink frothing over the fence and the Cat
House. She thrusts her branches across the path, catching
the unwary in her thorny embrace to such effect that I have
to attempt to bludgeon her into submission. It's not that I
want to frustrate their splendour, but 'Blush Noisette' and
'Rambling Rector', as well as 'Blushing Lucy', have such a
zest for life that the walls of the garden are on the point
of being toppled.

Not all the roses like being here, and this baffles me
because up until now I have maintained (and still do)
that roses are the most agreeable of plants and will grow
in contrary soils – in clay, limestone, loam, and even in
arid unwatered parts of Europe. Yet here 'Souvenir du
Dr Jamain', 'Desprez à fleurs jaunes', 'Rose de Resht'
and so on are among those that have remained sickly
and I can't understand why. However, I won't give up
on them; I know that if I change their position or hang
on for another year, they are quite as likely to suddenly
take off and never look back.

No doubt the fashion will turn full circle and it'll not
be long before we're incited to return to growing Hybrid
Teas and Compact Floribundas in mounded, weed-free
beds where each rose keeps its distance from the next. At
present the trend is still to have roses such as 'The Fairy' in
among perennials, and to have old shrub roses supporting
the globular heads of alliums or spires of verbascums . . .
but the long-condemned 'Dorothy Perkins' is definitely on
the rebound.

If I knew where garden trends were heading, I might run in the other direction. Nothing is more dispiriting than to go into a shop to buy a particular garment and be told by the assistant that 'these are very popular this season' – so are baseball caps worn back-to-front. The fickle fashion for what's accepted and what is not in the horticultural world should be disregarded. I know dahlias are in the ascendancy, red-hot pokers are old hat, and monkey-puzzle trees are about to make a comeback; Jekyll borders are *outré*, and wild gardens have been on the rampage for far too long. But who cares? Why bother with trends, fashions, conformity and good taste – whatever that is? Go for what turns you on, and in that way there's hope that the same repetitive planting won't be thrust down our throats on television and in magazines *ad infinitum.* The swing of fashion is tedious: how much better to be as unconforming as women's clothes have become. Once the vagaries of the hemline were rigidly adhered to, resulting in a tiresome annual alteration to the length of our skirts. That's all over now; we wear any length of garment we prefer, and it should be the same with gardens.

I dread the day scientists invent everlasting plants – it's bad enough having strawberries at Christmas – yet I see nothing wrong with spreading synthetic grass on a city rooftop garden. Artificial snow is now siphoned onto mountains; fake logs keep our sitting rooms blazing; and one gardener in this town has hand-made roses all over his pergola. I won't go that far myself because, although the loss of blackspot wouldn't break my heart, walking in the garden where there were no scents certainly would. Why grow a thing if the scent of it, defining one of the seasons of the year, is lacking?

An Enigma

But this brings me to the great gardening conundrum. Why aren't smokers honest? They might just as well say outright, on entering this garden in midsummer, 'Heavens, what is that dreadful smell? Ah, roses! And, my God, philadelphus and pinks, too?' Instead they prevaricate; they say things like: 'Oh, what fragrance. How I love the scents of summer.' Unfortunately, I'm no longer fooled. I used to be, but now I know better. Within a few minutes, to overcome the smells of a summer garden, they light up. It's worse if we sit down: that's asking for smokers to get out their cigarettes and lighter. As we take the seat under the honeysuckle and the heavy heads of 'Blairi No. 2', the whole lot, the flowery scents I mean, go up in smoke. And it's as bad after rain, when the fragrance of flowers is heightened; then they don't sit down because the bench is wet, and instead we walk along paths, following in their slipstream. Blindfold I could trace their route as the lingering trace of nicotine twists through the garden like an invisible thread.

It's as if they find garden scents abhorrent, yet I've not come across one smoker who has the honesty to say so; nor do I understand their protestations of love of gardens, any more than I can understand those who light up between courses but swear they are gourmets. Chefs complain of punters who wear strong perfume in their restaurants when they could be enjoying aromatic smells: I feel that in my garden, carrion under the rose 'Madame Isaac Pereire' and pig slurry under the jasmine would go unnoticed by those with smoke curling up their nostrils. And what happens when they are faced with the one plant above all others they should love, the starry flowers that fill the evening with fragrance and that loom white and ghostly in the dusk – do they then, finally, throw away their cigarettes? I mean, of course, *Nicotiana sylvestris*, the trumpet-shaped tobacco flower whose heavy scent wafts through the air bringing a breath of Argentina and voluptuous surrender to even the most poisoned pair of lungs. And no, they don't.

But yes, of course some of my best friends are smokers, and will go on being so – friends, and smokers. My youngest daughter is one; my son and son-in-law are too. It amounts to going to a concert wearing ear-plugs because the music is unbearable, but it's such fun watching the tympanist. A French gardener told me that at a grand international gardening conference she heard a distinguished British garden owner speak despairingly of the sight of *hoi polloi* walking past his exquisitely subtle herbaceous borders wearing rancid colours. After the symposium, my friend suggested to the speaker that his anguish could be resolved by supplying visitors with cotton cloaks in co-ordinated colours. Thinking her mad he backed off, but it was a practical solution: after all, tourists in Greece are handed bits of drapery to conceal their bare limbs before entering a monastery.

Where will this garden go next? I'm not sure. All I know is that it won't remain static. No garden does. But as I discover how the plants behave among themselves, I shall adapt myself accordingly. Nothing is forever, and in gardens this fact is discernible. Recently I met a man who said he was moving on; he was bored with his garden: 'I've done everything. I've made it.' Done everything? In a garden? I couldn't understand his language. A garden is something with its own impetus and life force; it alters before your eyes. I can understand how some gardeners move on in search of a kinder climate, a different soil and terrain; or why people who like doing up houses keep moving. But boredom? With a garden?

Circumstances and not boredom made me move, and now that I have I enjoy my new quandaries. Yet I know that if I had stayed with the old garden, there too I would still be transplanting things, making another wall, or spreading the bulbs further and further into countryside where the hundreds of broad-leafed trees Michael and I planted are by now filling parts of the sky.

CHAPTER IV

Growing to Love the Plants I Hate

There is no plant that doesn't merit a second look. Take the dandelion for instance: pick a bunch of them in spring and stuff them so closely together that they form a brilliant yellow pincushion standing in a blue clay pot, and I defy anyone to say they look awful. The arrangement may not be classy, but the flowers do look brazen and jaunty and well worth rescuing from the mower. When we lived in the Far East, my Thai friends would have been enchanted to receive a clump of dandelions, such recherché flowers, wildly foreign and exotic compared to the common bougainvillaea and hibiscus which surrounded them. 'These I've brought you are so English,' I would have promised them, 'with elegant cut leaves and the prettiest of seed-heads.' Conversely, my neighbours in Thailand couldn't understand our passion for canna lilies, which to them were merely vulgar.

As for gladioli, one stem standing stately and immobile in a narrow-necked bottle on a window sill with light shining through the petals becomes a work of art. Look closely, and all the unyielding awkwardness of them growing in a flower bed falls away. Look again: see how precisely the furled buds are arranged on the stem, and the throats of meretricious colours in the open flowers. Who in their senses would dare to make fabric – silk or lawn, say – with blood-red blotches on a jaundiced yellow background? What inartistic buffoon would put together anything as lurid as frilly ginger florets filled with dollops of maroon? I ask you – given a piece of paper and a paintbrush, would *you*? Only a child has the ingenuousness to put colours together like this, and yet with gladioli – one of the most engineered plants in our gardens – artlessness is just what you will get. Assuming that you cannot bring yourself to grow them, go out and buy a few, separate the bunch, stand just one of these 'artefacts' in a vase, and tell me that the brash configuration of the flower isn't utterly and wildly superb.

What all this is leading up to is my contention that there's no intrinsic beauty to flowers. I dislike rhododendrons – they do nothing for me – yet I adore oleanders. Why? What's the difference? Not much, really, and furthermore many Greeks can't bear oleanders – coarse and common is how they regard them. It's all a matter of our own personal taste and that, for sure, is utterly wayward and can alter at any time. There is no defining absolute. Looked at with other eyes, every flower has its own singularity. Bindweed may be a thug but it can also be a godsend, coming at a time of year when its fresh whiteness and delicate flowers revive a slouching garden. Only the bindweed's invasiveness makes us send it packing while other trespassers – aquilegias or heartsease – may remain inviolate.

I believe that one can do anything with anything: an ugly house can be changed by false shutters, or a badly-proportioned room improved by blocks of colour; a man's shirt can be turned into a woman's by taking off the collar and changing the buttons; ancient bed springs are ideal as plant supports; love-birds on French net curtaining make a romantic wedding dress; and a *trompe-l'oeil* on a blank wall outside the basement window can distract you at the sink. Years ago in Greece the large wooden donkey saddles that are ridden sideways used to be lined with a mixture of sheep and goats' fleece woven on narrow looms into a dense grey, cream and brown tweed perfect, I found, for making into a cloak. The stuff has a primitive earthiness about it, and a slight scent of ungulate still lingers in its folds. (No one weaves the material any more: red plastic has replaced it, to the detriment of the donkeys at the height of summer.)

This chapter is a challenge to myself to prove my own argument. However much I may dislike or even loathe certain plants, any one of them, used in a different way, can be given space in my garden. This particular garden is an imaginary place rather than a factual one, because unfortunately I haven't the time to construct tangible proof of what I'm talking about. I'm out to test my theory that it's only an attitude of mind that turns us away from some plants while we embrace others with unwavering commitment.

GROWING TO LOVE THE PLANTS I HATE

The garden I am about to make is in my mind, and all the ingredients that go into its creation will be things I wouldn't include from choice – the living or inert components that I have long considered ugly, whether plant or furniture, statuary, paving or pots. This nightmare place will have to contain some of the names gathered over years on my ever-changing plant Hit List: flowers that I've passed over, turned my back on, condemned to floral euthanasia or hissed at with an uncharitable lack of benevolence based merely on prejudice. These plants haven't had a chance up until now. Some I haven't known how to cope with, others I've been too impatient to cultivate. Now every judgement will be stood on its head, and I'll make the best I can from what I've always thought the worst.

As I've acknowledged from the start that it's merely an attitude of mind that has kept me looking with a preconceived bias, now that I'm facing in another direction each tree, shrub or flower that I'm about to plant will be treated with respect. I don't want to send them up; I want to grow them in earnest, in the best possible way that I can devise. They may not be erogenous zones exactly but I hope that the results will be ravishing, spectacular, or at the least pleasantly charming. The garden of course is sheer fantasy; I haven't the foggiest idea how it would work in reality but probably hundreds of you have, and may well be enraged by my guesswork, by my misinformation, and my mistiming. I can only apologise for getting it wrong, and remind you that I'm writing this chapter from my imagination, not from practice.

Obviously the easiest way to grow dubious plants would

be to keep them in groups of the same colour, so that their lack of charisma would be diffused; but I feel this would be a cop-out, and as I've made my own rules and challenged myself, I mustn't cheat. This has to be an exercise in making a garden, as pleasing a garden as possible, rather than simply laying out a spectrum of colours arranged in beds.

A Garden in the Mind

I shall begin with a piece of furniture against which I've waged an ongoing fatwa for years: a jumbo-sized Lutyens garden bench (designed by him for Lady Sackville's Brighton garden) covered all over in glossy white paint. In other colours the classic bench looks superb. 'The common habit of painting garden seats a dead white is certainly open to criticism,' wrote Gertrude Jekyll as long ago as 1918. 'The seat should not be made too conspicuous. Like all other painted things about a garden: gates, railings, or flower-tubs, the painting should be such as to suit the environment; it should in no case be so glaring as to draw almost exclusive attention to itself.'

Hallelujah to that wise lady, whose principles concerning colour are still valid today, although our choices now are far greater than she could lay her hands on.

However, as I have to have it – the glaringly white bench – I'll do my best to make it look jolly by planting red-hot pokers (torch lily is a prettier name) to thrust up through the slats. Assuming that some people will have the audacity to sit here, they'll need to push aside the spikes and perch in their summer garments surrounded by flaming lances. But what shall I plant around the seat? I feel that whites or off-whites would be the only tones that wouldn't detract from the drama, so a tangle of common white jasmine interlaced with that great fat many-petalled clematis, 'Duchess of Edinburgh', would be grown together on trellis at the back and on either side of the seat, at a slight distance from it so as not to crowd Lutyens. But these two climbers have never been on even my Second Division Hit List, so I think I ought instead to choose the passion flower, a climber I've given up on because I seem to always get far too much foliage and far too few short-lived flowers which never anyway look anything like the exquisitely intricate plants that grow in the tropics.

The six or more people sitting on this over-generous bench in a row – a formation that kills conversation stone dead – will face the most enormous kidney-shaped pool in which will be floating hybrid water-lilies of spectacular size and colour. 'Escarboucle' will be carefully restrained, so that on sunny days blobs of brilliant blue sky will be reflected to contrast with the lilies' crimson flowers six or eight inches in diameter. On one side a thicket of bamboo twenty feet high will make a continual sibilance or rattle, according to the breeze. Among the prefabricated 'stone' slabs surrounding the pool I shall leave gaps in which to plant varieties of *Coleus blumei*, whose shades will harmonize with the water-lilies. They may not make it through the winter, but if they do, the overall scene will be congenial. The appearance of the pool could be greatly improved if the surrounding slabs were to overhang somewhat, making a shadowy margin where the water, being invisible at the edges, would look as though it were flowing away underground.

Beyond the pool I must tackle the subject of island beds. What's wrong with them? Why should they be condemned? And how can they be made to take on a rhythmic movement that will enhance the general flow of the garden, rather than looking like a bad attack of acne spattering the sward? I think what I must do is to join all mine with ribbons of narrow beds to bind the islands together. But what shall I plant in these ribbons? Heather, of course – the visceral and scrubby stuff that should only be seen through mist on distant Scottish highlands, but never in a garden. Here, lying in unobtrusive skeins loosely twisting round the islands, the heather will work as a background to threads of grey-blue *Clematis jouiniana* 'Praecox' or one of the herbaceous clematis, *C. heracleifolia*, with their clusters of hyacinth-like flowers: up until this moment, I've never been able to use either of these purposefully in the garden. Here they will find their niche, but they won't be allowed to be unruly: I want the scalpel-sharp edges of both the island beds and the heather beds to appear clearly defined in a velvet sward such as every professional gardener would die for. Not a worm-cast or mole-heap, no daisy, clover, speedwell or moss will show itself across green lawns where the dead straight marks of the mower will add interest to its peerless texture.

When I was more agile than I am now I fantasized about making small gardens based on embroidery designs from other centuries, using different plants for the different stitches found in crewel work, samplers, Gobelins,

Florentine, and so on. Life is kinder than you think: my bones may creak but at last, and without bending my knees, my island beds offer me the prospect of following this thread of thought. What shall I choose to put in them? Here is a chance to buy up all those cheery little plants heaped in wheelbarrows outside garden centres and use them to form appliqué patterns in colours of unimagined fluorescence. But where shall I start? The choice is overwhelming. Perhaps if I go for inspiration to Ottoman or Caucasian sources, to their rugs, paintings and embroideries, I can give each bed a different design in which an intricate overall pattern is created from flowers used repeatedly with exquisite formality.

A Shiraz '*mille-fleurs*' prayer rug could be the inspiration for a dense planting of bright-faced pansies in which the balance of certain repetitive colours gives the bed cohesion. In another a variegated ivy would be used as tambour chain-stitching round each daisy-like orange *Sanvitalia procumbens*, thus redeeming these creeping zinnias – things I abhor, but here, with my profounder and more lingering gaze, I shall see them as a piece of fabric from Tartary. In a third bed there will be that bronze and green ground-cover perennial *Trifolium repens* 'Purpurascens' – surely in itself a name to send out bad vibes? – but here mine will be grown in patterns with that fat, glossy succulent, *Sedum obtusatum*. I find it quite repulsive because it reminds me of cats' innards and of the laboratory at school where, in a sickening smell of formaldehyde, we had a biology class on dissection. If it doesn't work, this island bed will be unobtrusive enough to be overlooked by those too fastidious to stomach the sight.

I shall have to have one circular bed jammed full of St John's wort, a large genus which includes that dismal thing with the beautiful name, the Rose of Sharon. These plants always seem to be resorted to as blotting paper to suck up space when the gardener has run out of ideas, in just the same way as chefs use a *coulis* when they are stuck for a bit of runny colour. '*Si on ne sait pas, on fait le coulis!*' said one chef when I was researching restaurants in France for a book. I loved his honesty in admitting that when he was stumped he would pass something through a fine sieve and spoon it all over the plate. The Rose of Sharon is a gardener's *coulis.* The plant is as dispiriting as Morris dancers. My dislike of it has never wavered, yet now that I'm going to use the Rose of Sharon possibly the rotundity of the cup-shaped yellow flowers will contrast with the slender spikes of the pink hebe, 'Great Orme'. And because I'm taking this bed seriously, the composition of hypericums and hebes shall be framed by a frill of the poached-egg flower, *Limnanthes douglasii,* used as though it were a thick silk border taken from a piece of Bokhara embroidery.

Once you've started, there could be no end to the uses to which you might put a wheelbarrow full of feisty garden-centre plants.

Trees and Rockeries

Trees. The challenge to find the unloveliest of trees must, naturally, start with cherries (*pace* Housman). They'll be exiled to a secluded orchard where the drooping branches of a dozen deep pink flowering *Prunus* 'Kiku-shidare' will alternate with columns of the upright semi-double pink *P.* 'Amanogawa'. I might not pull off this pattern of contrastingly-shaped trees, because with no experience of actually growing them I'm not sure that their flowering in spring will overlap, but at least in autumn their unison of leaves should create a visual bonfire. As for *P.* 'Fukubana' – well, doesn't it deserve a place on its own? With its rose-madder, semi-double flowers, this small tree shall rise out of a tablecloth of densely planted purple crocus. Imagine it. Like butterflies to buddlejas we'll be drawn across the garden to stand in awe at this improbable sight.

Few are likely to agree with my inclusion of forsythia on the Hit List, but I find its colour far too strident at this time of year, when it dominates everything for miles around. The colours of spring are so tender: the greens, apricots and primrose yellows, the soft blues and mild lilacs. The only way I'll have it here is kept open and lacy, against a stone wall – the yellow of Cotswold stone rather than Kidderminster puce.

What other brutes must I cope with? Well, there are the variegated hollies, I suppose. I've thought and thought about them. How can I integrate those rotters with 'Aurea' after their names into the garden? If I'm to prove my point that it's only the capriciousness of taste that makes me hate them, I must use all my ingenuity. I know: maybe if I scatter mats of aromatic origanum, *O. vulgare* 'Aureum', around the small holly *Ilex aquifolium* 'Ovata Aurea' there'll be a certain bonding between the two. Perhaps. But to distract me from pausing here too long, nearby there'll be a shallow gully flanked on either bank by a rockery.

Rockeries. What's wrong with rockeries? Why have I continually shied away from them? Worse still, I haven't even given them a second thought. My defence is that having once seen plants growing naturally among stones and scree on mountain sides or at the base of cliffs along a seashore, then every effort I could make would seem to me to be downhill all the way. The short-lived flowering of certain plants, their fragility, vivid colours and tenacity for life under catastrophic conditions, are touching and miraculous: in a desert it may be years before rain brings dormant seeds into flower, and among mountain peaks the roots of alpines can live for many seasons under snow until it melts enough to allow them to bloom. In fact, their determination to survive is so fierce that some alpines even generate enough warmth to melt the last trace of snow cover. If ever Dylan Thomas's poem 'The Green Fuse that Drives the Flower' were apt, it must be here in the harsh wilderness of mountainous terrain.

The exciting way to grow these plants would be in a natural setting of rocky outcrops on your land. The provocation then would be irresistible. Or should you be fortunate enough to get your hands on a collection of rectangular stones to lay on a raised low stone wall running along a path, I can then imagine what fun it would be to fill the crevices with rock plants. As I have not had access to either of those means and there are so many other floral distractions, rockeries have never been on my shopping list. Until this moment, I haven't even been curious enough to look for them in other gardens;

if your perceptions aren't sharp, it's only too easy to pass by, seeing only those things you've set your heart on. Could a rockery be integrated into a garden among things like topiary, herbaceous flower beds, temples, wisteria walks, knot gardens, octagonal arbours and espaliered trees? Or, like auriculas, do they need their own theatre?

Our ancestors were mad about rock gardens. No Victorian or Edwardian garden was acceptable without its rockery, using stone from whatever source. These bogus alpine habitats were contrived with fastidious care and botanical expertise. I did read of one that really went over the top: with extravagant insanity, tons of rock were used to re-create the Matterhorn. I can't compete. Here my imaginary rockery will be down-market, made from manufactured material. But amid profuse plantings of prostrate *Origanum* 'Kent Beauty', which will trail like unstitched bedroom flounces among the 'rocks', no one will notice the deceit. White candytuft and potentilla, stout-branched pink polygonum and crimson saxifrage will cover the synthetic ravine. To fit into the rest of the garden's persona there'll be squibs of one of those lurid magenta geraniums with black eyes. I'd have hebes too, the ones with melancholy mauve spikes, and another that doesn't warm the cockles either, *H. cupressoides.* Plump cushions – growing larger every year – of *Sedum acre* 'Aureum' interplanted with clumps of the taller *Mitella breweri* will ensure there'll be some sort of alliance between the lot. But I don't think this area is one I'll point out to visitors with pride.

Succulents; there's a word to either dry your mouth or liven up the responses. Yet I don't see why something so repulsively rousing shouldn't be included in this garden of the mind. Here in a sheltered and stony corner there'll be a small greenhouse just for them. Growing in their miniature desert I'll have glossy hairy mounds of gangrenous tones. With their weird and macabre forms, their 'spineless areoles', 'swollen branches', 'velvety finger-like leaves' or 'sunken fissures at their tips', these plants belong to a grotesque world I'm unable to enter. The loss is mine; but there we are, it's too late now.

Conifers and Other Unlovable Things

With few exceptions I've always steered clear of conifers, but now with my different set of eyes I'm going to use evergreens to dramatize the distance. Using closely-planted alternate blue and golden conifers, left to grow as tall as possible before being cut into crenellations and kept impeccably neat, I shall construct an impregnable wall along one of the boundaries. Monkey-puzzle trees used to give me the creeps with their reptilian branches, but here I shall have an avenue of them. As they are slow growers no one need ever be around long enough to face the result of this folly, and in their youth the trees' symmetrical habit and spiralling leathery leaves will make a bizarre corridor down which few will be tempted to venture. But if you are, at the far end you will find a prefabricated, metal, octagonal gazebo bought in a garden centre, and it will contain metal benches. The whole structure will be painted the colour of rust, so that you can sit in it with the clashing strands of scarlet *Tropaeolum speciosum* insinuating itself all over the place. This is a herbaceous climber which I've never grown, though it's seen everywhere. Clambering over yew hedges like a stray piece of thread that needs picking off, it's a gardening cliché that leaves me cold, but there's a chance that here the abrasive combination of flame and rust will bowl me over.

Away from the margins of the garden and leading off my pristine lawn with its island beds there will be divisions to allow me to experiment with some of the plants I'm attempting to love. Are there, for instance, any plummy plants I like? Because of my instinctive revulsion from them they've long been condemned to the Hit List, yet my response is dependent on such a minute degree of colour variation – it only takes a subtle shift to something browner to lift the tone to that of a copper beech tree. My own dark *Pittosporum tenvifolium* 'Purpureum', whose leaves when young are green, turns in maturity to a glossy black-bronze a hair's-breadth away from being banished from my real garden.

I try to think that the smoke tree, *Cotinus coggygria* 'Royal Purple', is tolerable, but only if it's allowed to 'smoke', which is like a cosmetic over a wino's complexion. Might these shrubs have any merit? Possibly, if a group of them so closely planted they made one huge purple boulder (by mistake I typed 'blunder') were covered with a tangle of the unravelling orange trumpet flowers of the Chilean glory flower, *Eccremocarpus scaber* – they would clash so horribly the effect would be stunning.

What hedging shall I use? How I've loathed golden box, especially when it's planted in enormous blocks of hideosity. But no, I'll tackle another enemy. What have I really detested but which I must somehow now integrate to prove my theory? I don't think I can possibly go wrong with regularly pruned *Berberis thunbergii atropurpurea*. Its dismal oppressiveness will hold down the begonias, bergenias, crocosmias, dahlias and zinnias. I must say a word about the last-named: looking as manufactured as dahlias, they shall be included here as stippled, bleached coral or unhealthy greenish-white blemishes infecting the other flowers. If they are used as loners, given time I might even come to like their subtle colours.

The framing of these compartments is to be uncompromising; strong and single-coloured, as if a dark crayon had been used to outline them. There'll be paths of black gravel instead of grass. (A vivid green would emasculate the flowers and the place might look dreadful.) In some areas deep crimson double begonias will pick up the sombre depth of the hedging, but to keep any discordant flowers from looking too hysterical the beds will be in semi-shade, from a disparate planting of trees outside the hedges yet close enough to cast an ever-moving pattern of shadows across the beds.

Light is so critical to the intensity of colour that it changes a mood. It can goad or placate my responses, so that at certain times of day I feel like backing off while at others I'm willingly pulled under. See how a group of the dahlia 'Sunny Boys' can change from being abusive in full sunshine to benign in shadow. With dahlias in particular I know I must make a great leap into space, stop dragging my feet, look again, and forget how in France their raw voltage fused whole gardens.

I must expunge memories of bad trips, acknowledge my hang-ups, and with an unjaundiced eye look at the perfect symmetry of the dahlias' flower types, the decorative, semi-cactus and ball, the pompom and collarette. Yes, on further scrutiny, and going in the opposite direction to the one my instinctive responses spring from, I do admire their forms. Some pink ones (the cactus) look like sea anemones, others (the pompom) could be used as buttons to fasten a velvet cloak in theatricals; some have scrolled petals of metallic precision, others have bright yellow centres surrounded by a choirboy collar of white. In my garden I'm determined to have the opulently red 'Comet' (anemone) dahlias which will clash spitefully, but triumphantly, with the hedging. There will be no yellows, whites or pinks, but shaggy orange ones to give an air of untidiness amid all the mathematically precise forms in crimson, copper and vermilion. To modulate their regimented personae I'd like to use clumps of spear-leafed red and orange crocosmias haphazardly rising from their midst, but never having grown any of these flowers I'm not sure how their heights will combine. Oh well, what does it matter? I'll give it a go, and if it doesn't work I'll change the arrangement next year.

The bergenias I've got it in for are puce, or something like that nasty colour on our Judas trees in Greece, their lurid encrustations appearing before the leaves had a chance to soften the disfiguring scabs. It wasn't the trees that made my spirit shrivel – it was the colour. Here I'll tackle the problem by hiding the puce bergenias in one of the compartments far from the delicate colours of spring. Later in the year another of the compartments will explode with tuberous begonias – the kind I find utterly, unshakeably unlovely. I think, taken head on, these flowers could be as prismatic as a stroboscope at a disco. Each gargantuan face will upstage anything you will see at the Hampton Court Flower Festival.

Tubers, corms, bulbs and rhizomes span a gamut of flowers from the loveliest to the most brash. As I've condemned myself to banish erythoniums, lilies, snowdrops and winter aconites, among the many others that I lost my heart to years ago, I haven't a hope of mitigating the awfulness of some of the flowers I have chosen. But it's astonishing how fleshy stems, hairy leaves or crimson veins can set me quivering, and how by taking another course and finding that 'creeping' and 'rootstock' are agreeably positive words, I can go a long way to convincing myself to see these plants from a different slant.

There Must Be a Patio

No garden worth its salt should be without a patio. Well, no garden of this particular genre. My self-imposed brief is to make this area, constructed of coloured gravel, purple bricks and precast concrete, as handsome as possible. It will spread out from the French windows as neat and clean as a sheet of unwritten paper. No morsels of earth in which grass might seed will fill the cracks; no pelt of moss will be allowed to spread over it in winter. Instead of choosing polystyrene Greek urns, which have a natural affinity with patios, I'll choose instead large square planters made of the same white plastic as the patio table and chairs. But using white plastic chairs in a garden is unforgivable. Anywhere. If you have to have plastic chairs and table, then paint them. It's quite possible if you use an Acrylic Convertor as a primer before using whatever paint you choose, and then cover it with non-yellowing matt varnish, which will protect even a water-based paint.

To create visual unity the furniture, the trellis, the pots and the planters will all be painted the same colour. I learned the benefit of this from the use of blue in the late Nancy Lancaster's garden at Haseley Court. The continuity of the same colour throughout her gardens was the same as if her voice were accompanying you everywhere. Here I shall use a really good yellow – not a rinsed-out primrose nor a hard chrome – that has the appearance of having been around for a long time from looking slightly soiled. By including a trace of green and possibly a speck of black, these undertones should create a manky yellow to blend with plants, stone and brick and, of course, a swinging seat with its co-ordinated canopy.

Purple and yellow when combined are trenchant colours. The purple flowers will pick up on the broken-veins complexion of the bricks framing the patio and the fountain, which will have the plastic pots grouped round its base rather than being lined up at regular intervals. The wild toadflax that creeps so prettily out of walls is welcome in my real garden, but I don't really lust after its three-foot-high relation, *Linaria triornithophora*, a spiky purple and yellow flower that has a curmudgeonly disposition. Here the linaria, growing in pots, will be a paler, softer, more diffused hue than the brash *Clematis* 'Jackmanii Superba' festooning the trellis. This clematis with its jumbo-sized flowers has been on my Hit List from the moment when I first saw it among the marvellous collection Raymond Evison had at Treasures Nursery, near Tenbury Wells in Shropshire, many years ago. It was then that I lost my heart to the small, to the nodding, to the greenish-white and the bell-shaped clematis, with their clandestine characteristics. Between them, they are a gift to gardeners for more than half the year. But now along the trellis and mixing with the 'Jackmanii Superba' I'll have a plummy mauve 'Kathleen Windsor' with flowers the size of a saucer. A jumbo flower. A mega-bloom. My, what a rich, extravagant vision they will make together tumbling over the yellow trellis. I can't wait for summer.

It's here on the patio that I need to face my aversion to variegated plants, and I shall do so by using a few pots of tender *Iresine herbstii* 'Aureoreticulata', the Beefsteak plant with bloody veins, standing at the foot of the tall variegated hebe, *H.* × *andersonii* 'Variegata', with its spikes of mauve flowers. (I wonder which Mr Anderson it was who thought the plant worth bringing back from New Zealand, when that country has the most fascinating collection of native treasures to choose from?)

What am I to do with a poinsettia and a coleus? With a name so lyrical as 'poinsettia' you feel you can't go wrong. But I knew them far too intimately in the Far East, and came increasingly to dislike their straggly growth and red bracts – the sort of colour that doesn't 'breathe' – growing at the ends of bare sticks. At present I'm mentally carrying the poinsettia and coleus round this garden, as Vita Sackville-West used to do with some of her plants as she searched for the right surroundings. Both of mine are greenhouse plants, but I'm looking for a suitable background against which the pots could be comfortably camouflaged in summer. No, on second thoughts, perhaps not. I think I'll jam them back into the greenhouse, well concealed behind the banana tree which I have absolutely no ambition to grow.

'Glauca' – that's a word that can make my hackles rise. I do like grasses, but *Festuca glauca* generates a certain wariness, and anyway something described in a catalogue as having 'spikelets' has to be bad news. However, this grass, growing in gravel with other grasses, and with variegated ivies groping and sidling at their feet, will give the effect of bilious tones interspersed with silver and blue – it won't be half bad. What ivies? Well, if I'm patient *Hedera helix* 'Sagittifolia', but if I'm in a hurry then it had better be *H. colchica* 'Dentata Variegata'. Both are horrible, and both have been permanent residents of the Hit List, but here I hope the variegation in stance and texture of the grasses and the ivy will somewhat mitigate their unloveliness. In this imaginary exercise, the ivies will go into orbit round a central clump of pampas grass erupting like a geyser from among the smaller plants.

Roses and Fuchsias

It's blast-off time in the rose bed. This vast genus is as explosive as seeds on a caper spurge, whether it's the beauty of a dog-rose making your hair stand on end or a bed of hybrids giving you an instant migraine. Whatever happens, you can't be unresponsive; no one can shrug off these garden inhabitants as trivia. Everybody must have some sort of opinion when confronted by a rose. I've been very stuffy about them. From the first I found the kinds I wanted, and I never looked further. Perhaps I should have. Perhaps there is a world beyond the Albas, Gallicas, Damasks and Centifolias.

I must sharpen my perceptions, look again, and consider how I would deal with roses that up till now have never caused me to shorten my step. I've walked by with my mind intent on Bourbons and Chinas, on Rugosas and Portlands, and not once paused before Hybrids, Miniatures and Floribundas.

Whatever the rose, I see no merit – except accessibility – in growing each shrub in its own desert of bare earth. My copper 'Just Joey' won't: it will be surrounded by the softer tones of the potentilla 'Day Dawn', which will merge into the orange, red and yellow of 'Remember Me' and 'Piccadilly' roses, with their glossy leaves and lack of blackspot and scent. That absence doesn't matter. My childhood was spent being told I couldn't have everything. These roses will be my nemesis. And anyway, I'm informed that 'Mountbatten' is reasonably fragrant, and the colour of his yellow clustered flowers will seep gently into 'Champagne Cocktail', whose pink edges will pick up and carry me on towards fuchsias, plants I've never known where to place. And even more, I'm not sure, once I have them in the garden, whether I'll like them. There are so many flowers that are instinctive integraters; you can put them almost anywhere, they can be used to muddle, confuse, soften, outline or flatter any one of the divas in the garden. Fuchsias are not in this class.

Yet for a long time now they have intrigued me. Partly because I can't unravel my feelings about them – except for those pink ones with silver and pinkish leaves. It's the others that leave me hesitant. What do you do with them? How should they be grown? Once, in a small town near me, I visited a garden belonging to a fuchsia freak. She grew nothing else; she had them everywhere, in beds and troughs, in pots on the ground, along low walls, on window sills, and even on the garden table, where they barely left space for a bottle and glasses. The sight was pulverizing; and as she showed me around I expected each plant we passed to emit little tinkly sounds. Can such things be taken seriously? What, with those colours? With that degree of ornateness? Heavens, some were enough to raise your scalp. Others were just lurid; but some were as elaborate as oriental *bijouterie*. They certainly didn't belong to the great out-of-doors, to the buffeting elements, to the thrust and shove of inclement weather. A few were peerless, and I would gladly have walked off with them.

A BREATH FROM ELSEWHERE

I've pondered long on this quandary: where, if I did have fuchsias, would I grow them? In the past, and long before I was taking the question seriously, I did consider planting them among roses. But I could never imagine their chichi appearance in the same arena as my great classic shrub roses. Now at last, with a Garden in the Mind, there's a chance they will find their vocation.

I'll try a few 'Dollar Princess' fuchsias, whose upright stance and cerise-red tubes and purple sepals will bring a contrary deportment into the bed. If I plant it with two-foot-tall 'Sexy Rexy', a double and fragrant rose whose pink is more suitably blue than that of 'Keepsake', the two opposing definitions might work: I do like the idea of the alternating shapes, the cupped flowers of the roses surrounded by the pendulous tassels with the splayed sepals of the fuchsias. The bed may need some blobs of black to prevent it from suicidal lift-off. The fuchsia 'Gruss aus dem Bodethal' might be used here, with crimson flowers which do have a blackish appearance. Black tulips and fritillaries come far too early in the year, black hollyhocks would be too tall – but would the viola 'Bowles' Black' work as groundcover for these pantomime performers? Alternatively, some ecclesiastical deep purple alliums might, and perennial geraniums, *G. phaeum* 'Mourning Widow', *Cosmos atrosanguineus* with its black-crimson sobriety, and the handsome and most sumptuous sweet William, *Dianthus barbatus* Nigrescens Group, could sober down the combustible atmosphere.

You can see how I'm slipping from the strictures I set myself: these near-black flowers have constantly been on my Most Wanted List. The time has come to stop coping with roses – the flower bed is getting too large. Except for a huddle of red 'Sheri Anne' miniatures crouching in the shade of the tasselled annual Love-lies-bleeding (more melodically known as amaranthus) – plants I don't warm to – and the even smaller and softer-toned 'Angela Rippon', I now intend to clear my head of rosy suffusions.

There is one last masochistic exercise to be undertaken. I began with a brilliant white Lutyens bench; I shall end with a swimming pool, my *bête noire*.

Visiting gardens in summer provokes thoughts that won't lie down: swimming pools, for instance. In France swimming pools are as prescribed as dahlias and, like them, they are situated in such a way that they haven't a chance of integrating into their surroundings. These excrescences outraged every garden in every region of France that I visited, no matter how classic and sophisticated the estate was. But why, oh why, need the pool be turquoise? – an abrasive, shrill colour that sucks the light from every plant within its compass. An imitation of the aquamarine of Mediterranean coasts, the colour doesn't work in gardens. And why should a small building for changing in be so unutterably functional and inelegant, so graceless and ungainly? I rail against these ill-proportioned buildings, standing beside pools like lurid scars: the more beautiful the garden, the more outrageous are the blemishes. But swimming pools can be made to look harmonious. It is possible. When a pool is painted black, the blue of the water turns to a dark green, varying in intensity according to the time of day. The pool then blends into the garden, adding an expanse of still water to reflect cloud and creating a flat dimension of alternating lustre in contrast to everything that moves.

As for what encompasses a pool, choice is all-important. I can see that it isn't a good idea to have towering trees – or any trees, for that matter – too close to the water. But it can't be beyond imaginative ingenuity to contrive wind shelters in the form of hedges, shrubs, trellis or walls to enclose the pool. And furniture. Surely wet bottoms can be accommodated on chairs of other than white plastic standing under gaudy striped awnings and umbrellas that may look fine along the Riviera; but in the gentle light of northern countries muted tones would be less obtrusive.

No compromises will be allowed here. The pool must be turquoise, backed by a 'pavilion' with a curved cocktail bar. In the deepening shadows of twilight the water will appear profound, turning the place into one of mystery and salubrious healing. The scent of white flowers, coming into their own at dusk, will overlay the chemical trace of chlorine lingering since midday about the loungers. Softly, softly, wait awhile for the arrival of great, silent, downy-winged moths, drawn towards the perfume of the flowers and the rosy light from a pair of gilded street lamps beckoning like sirens from across the garden. Oh yes, this strident pool will be deceptively transformed and as the umbrellas are put away and dew falls, even the clink of ice in glasses will have its merit in a garden on the edge of reality.

Postscript

Many readers with their own Hit Lists will disagree with my choice of plants for this garden. For surely the ones I've chosen to condemn must be beautiful in the eyes of someone? Other gardeners may be just irritated, feeling an urge to protest at what I'm doing. But remember – 'Growing to Love the Plants I Hate' is subjective and imaginary; it has the underlying serious premises not only that one can make anything out of anything, but that by facing in another direction everything you've repudiated up until now can be turned into some sort of splendour with its own character and merit.

As a rider to this chapter and in an effort to talk myself round about particular plants, I wonder whether I could do the reverse? Could I stop being partisan over certain things and instead stand back, keep my cool, and pass an objective eye over everything that has always made me acquisitive? There are times when maybe we ought to be able to take a rational stance. Could I anaesthetize ardour and, by being more receptive, change my permanent tilt towards certain plants and away from others? I'd like to. I'd like to branch out, and stop instinctively going for every flower that is single rather than double.

Having indulged in roses by planting them all over our land without a modicum of subtlety, I did try when I moved here to take a dispassionate attitude to them and think – Enough: there must be other shrubs that have equally good variations of demeanour, proportion, scent and deportment. This time the garden could contain some of the plants I've admired and hankered after for years but never grown.

Is plumbago one of them? We had it growing up to the eaves of a house in Greece where we once lived, where the plumbago – unwatered for months on end and growing on a rocky terrace facing south – thrived on being ignored. Its magnificent cool blue fell like a waterfall down the wall and we, never tired of walking there at the hottest hour of the day, momentarily imagined a breath of freshness moving through the stifling air. But growing it here? In Shropshire, with its dropping temperatures? No, I shall forgo the temptation. I would expect too much, and inevitably end up disappointed.

Another plant I admire but which comes nowhere near being feasible is an Australian tree fern, *Dicksonia antarctica*. Twenty feet high, evergreen, and like some Brobdingnagian ferny mass, it would look highly improbable in a garden a few miles from Wales. Anyway, how on earth would I get it into my hall for the winter? I already have a pepper tree, *Schinus molle*, that fills the hall from floor to ceiling during the months of winter. Because the tree was brought to me by a beloved friend, now dead, who sheltered the two-inch seedling all the way back from Portugal in October 1992, I do my utmost to keep the tree going. Now that it's a tree, drooping with feathery foliage and filling the middleground of the courtyard with its grace from May till October, I need to restrain it, like the rest of the trees in this garden. Kept caged in a tub on wheels, it's doomed to be manhandled into the house where it stands against the back door, preventing it from being opened till spring. If only winter didn't last so long. By about March the pepper tree is shedding most of its leaves, although by nature it's an evergreen. Such an unnatural habitat means that the panicles of creamy flowers only appear in September, never in time for beads of rosy-red fruit to develop. Ah, but pinch a young leaf and the aromatic tang of fresh pepper is spicy and pungent.

These exotics apart, there are more available things to go for. Tribes of lilies, delphiniums and irises, for instance; abutilons and lupins – perhaps. *Fremontia californica* and the self-adhesive schizophragma that I'd like to exchange my *Hydrangea petiolaris* for. And the cranesbill, 'Buxton's Blue' – I've long wanted to see their frank white eyes staring into the garden. The plant has a nomadic inclination to scramble into other things, in the same way as some campanulas. But why is this one so difficult to find in nurseries, compared to the ubiquitous 'Johnson's Blue'?

Imagine waking early in July to the sight of a blue morning glory, *Ipomoea tricolor* 'Heavenly Blue', twining up something outside the window. I think about it. I know their lives are brief, but their beauty is incomparable – a fact that makes them even more precious. Things that behave like butterflies, with the same frailty and the same transitory life-span, don't put me off trying to grow them. When a ceanothus flowers flat out for six weeks, or lily-flowered tulips span a whole springtime, or I read the word 'remontant' in connection with a rose, I'm elated; yet some of the plants that almost have one breath only are treasures. I adore them more for this, and find that their fleeting flowering is worth waiting for eleven and a half months of each year.

There used once to be edible treats in our lives as things came in and out of season, but now that strawberries are in the shops throughout the year and every chef cuts one in half to slap down beside the pudding even in winter, they are no longer summer treats to quicken a child's pace when they first appear in the garden. So it is with flowers. I've never wanted erythroniums to stay around until August. If the petals of *Rosa sancta* almost dissolve before my eyes, I don't condemn it.

Returning to where I started from, that there is no intrinsic beauty to a flower, has produced an unexpected spin-off. Working on this chapter meant that I've had to reappraise my own judgements, and that can't be a bad thing. My prejudices had become intractable, so much so that I had never troubled to evaluate them again but had accepted my original responses and stuck with them. Now, by looking hard at the design of dahlias, chrysanthemums, gladioli, tuberous begonias and even gloxinias, I've forced myself to be less stuffy.

CHAPTER V

Dead-Heading the Guilt

This chapter is for you, the people who are left behind. It is for those whose gardening life has been shared with some-one, even if one of you may never have dirtied your hands. There are gardeners whose wife or husband has offered years of appreciative and encouraging murmurings. Their constructive opinions served as a sounding board against which at times to push in opposition. But now, left in charge of something you may never have created in the first place, you find the garden is on your conscience and under your feet. You are the widows and widowers, the bereaved and solitary, left with a legacy that too often loads you down with guilt.

'I can't die because I have to see the crocuses next spring!' said a voice from the audience to whom I was showing slides. The sighs that arose after that gaunt statement showed how everyone there empathized with her remark. Of course she can't. As gardens are always in a state of flux, they keep us optimistically looking forward throughout the winter. This is both their charm and their power. Other than children, what is there in life that maintains our anticipation with such unwavering tunnel vision; something that's continually growing. Promotion? Applause? Fame? A knighthood?

But one of you will leave the garden first.

This aspect of gardening is never voiced. Is it that the words would be too harrowing for our sensibilities? That we don't want to know, or even think about it? Or is it that the matter is far too intrusive and personal to be brought up and discussed? Whatever the reason, we veer away, keeping the subject in the shadows. Instinctively and with a sense of self-preservation, we don't want to contemplate what no one puts into words. But I shall; I'm writing for all of you who may have inherited an heirloom you never sought, whether you were the prime gardener or merely the partner who sat under a honeysuckle making suggestions.

I was first made aware of these people when a librarian described to me the sight of distressed readers (particularly on wet days) anxiously looking for practical advice on 'what to do with the garden'. They might not personally have been the major influence in the garden's creation years earlier when they were two and both were agile, but now, when things have changed, the place looms outside the window with its seasonal cries for help. A man, his eyesight waning, remembered with what pleasure his wife gathered roses for the house each summer. For him now to neglect those bushes would be a kind of betrayal: he'd feel he was turning his back on her. 'It would be a form of forgetting,' he said. 'The garden is such a burden,' a woman, alone for two years, lamented as she looked out of the window in despair. 'I struggle because my husband loved the garden. Now, whenever I don't look after it, I feel overcome with remorse.' Another complained about the weekly chore of grass-cutting. 'My partner took such pride in the lawn. I'm kept awake worrying about all the mowing there is to be done.' She then added somewhat ruefully, 'No one remarks when the lawn is trim, but they do the moment it looks a mess!' One gardener explained that now he has had to take on those jobs that his wife used to do, he hasn't time to keep the grass and the edges in good shape. He was aghast when I suggested that he should get rid of the lawn. 'I simply couldn't. I'd feel guilty – and anyway, what would the neighbours think?'

Yes, indeed, what would they think? Judas? Traitor? Betrayer? Deserter? – or Sensible Fellow?

These cries of dolour are universal. Gardeners endure the onus of the place dragging like an anchor on their state of well-being. Compunction and self-reproach, along with that vile underminer, conscience, erode every aspect of their gardens. Unfortunately the feeling doesn't get better: as the place falls apart and the centre no longer holds, so the anguish intensifies. The flowers their companions once tended only seem to increase the sense of bereavement. In the town where I live I met a woman who told me how her husband had loved his lilies. 'He'd hate to see them neglected, but how can I cope?'

The answer, of course, is Don't try.

You and I may be facing the dying of the light, but

there's no need to look backwards because your gardening partner is no longer beside you. Remembering how it once looked, recalling shared endeavours, the bereaved prepare themselves for a poignancy that seasonally returns with the arrival of seed catalogues. Stuck in a time warp, you are unable to extricate yourself from a grief that seems only bearable if you keep things as they were. To make a change would seem brutal.

Even after seven years it's all too easy to find myself going down behind my eyes in an effort to recall something so beautiful that a trace of it has remained trapped in my memory since Michael died. In the recesses of the mind, a fragment can be brought out in midwinter when it's hard to resurrect a sense of place, of colour, or of scent. Looking at every shrub and tree, every rose and bulb, feeling jubilant or downcast at whatever success or disaster that was happening, used to be as commonplace as having our meals together. The garden was a shared indulgence; utterly selfish, ingrowing, and at times bewildering, because we could never believe in what we had done, nor could we come to terms with what the garden had done for us. Yet how fortunate that we had no inkling of what was to be the last time that we walked in the garden together. If we had, it would have been unbearable. As it is, I try to remember, but can't. The ritual perambulation was so familiar that nothing in particular made it memorable. No prophetic intimations made me drag my feet; we must have done just what we had always done, and for having no memory of the occasion I shall be forever thankful.

To those people who speak in distress about the guilt

they would feel if they were to give up the maintenance of their gardens, I'd say this: Move forward. Seek renewal from other sources. By jumping in the deep end rather than treading water, it *is* possible to do something radical. Make a garden on your own.

I know this to be true. Once I was alone I moved into another area. The last one had closed for ever, and it was imperative to lay the ghostly reminders and surreptitious hauntings that come when one is at one's most vulnerable. After a year of living with the garden that Michael and I had made, I changed direction. It may have been from necessity, not choice, but I knew I had no one to depend on but myself, that only I could decide whether to stick with remorse or move into a different environment.

Life is one long series of adjustments, and death, with its almost incomprehensible finality, is the major one. Gardeners can take a sort of inverted comfort from reminding themselves periodically that the intrinsic quality of a garden comes from the very fact that it *is* ephemeral. Whether there are two of you or you are on your own, the garden will change however much you may want to hold it petrified forever. As one year is never like another anyway, carry this a bit further and alter tack completely. By abandoning the past and shrugging it off like an old skin, you may not emerge quite as beautiful as a dragonfly, but you will emerge. It's not a betrayal, but a valediction.

I'm often asked, even after seven years, if I miss my garden. 'How could you bear to leave it?' and, sometimes, 'How can you endure going back there again?' The answer is not complicated. Everything is over; the garden that Michael and I made doesn't exist. A few roses and of course the trees remain, but the presiding character vanished as soon as we left. And it should be like this. A garden is personal; it can't be perpetuated, and it's madness and egotistical to think it can. The same will happen with the garden I now have. Immortality and gardens don't work. Whoever comes to live here may do just what I did: wait a year, or perhaps less, and then take the whole place apart. Garden shed, mirrors, trees, Cat House, tortured quince, eucryphia, the lot.

The bonds that tie you to your garden are not only the visible ones – the plants, the colour, walls, buildings, trees and water; there's something else, a claim on part of you that is hard to relinquish. A sad corollary to this is the case of a friend in France, whose concept of making her garden was radical; she was always going forward. But when she grew too old to care for the place she let go of both – her garden, and her life. Within two weeks of moving to a new house, she died. It was as though the vitality of the garden and her relationship to it were inseparable. And is this so strange? To pull things off with such good timing as this isn't always within our control, but those who knew her unique garden and indomitable spirit should only rejoice that she brought about what she would have most wanted – not to outlive her garden.

An artist's work is dispersed forever once a painting or a piece of sculpture has been bought. So is the actor's performance. The poet and writer keep their words extant; the composer can hear the work performed again and again; the architect's design remains *in situ*, the bridge-builder, the stonemason, the wood carver or clockmaker have visual evidence of their achievements. But not a gardener. This thought is pivotal to making a garden. It is also pivotal to the answer to the question, How could you bear to leave your garden?

What Michael and I made has now turned into something else as Tamsin and her family live there and put their own imprint on everything: 'Another kind of chaos' is how she describes it. I like it that way. Theirs is something new, creative, and the idea of trying to keep the garden as we made it would almost feel traitorous. Where Michael and I could please ourselves, Tamsin has young children. This immediately imposes conditions: the brook has had to be fenced off; the planting simplified; a sandpit, a swing, a paddling pool and so on have been incorporated, as well as a productive kitchen garden, soft-fruit bushes, new orchard trees, chickens, and one magnificent cockerel. The guiding spirit has been replaced by something much more practical, robust and youthful, and though some of the bulbs we planted do return each spring along with the blossom and pussy-willow buds near the stream, those who live there now have already made it their own.

So when people ask, 'But how could you bear to leave?', the answer is simple. The garden was then; and having no choice in the scheme of things there was no alternative but to move on. Whether you are like me and move away, or whether you remain living in the same place on your own, you absolutely cannot maintain the status quo.

How Others Cope

There are people whose gardens have been well known for
years from having appeared in magazines and books and
being open to the public. But with the loss of their partners
they have gone another way. After a year or two they have
moved elsewhere, to create new gardens. If you are one
of these and you have no one to help in its construction,
scupper all ambitious ideas. It really is possible to make a
garden from the most unpromising dimensions and aspect.
A man I know, left on his own, finally moved into a town,
where his garden is a verdant sentry-box as functional as
those kitchen galleys where, by swivelling on your heel,
you have everything to hand. There's room for just a table
and chairs. Against the walls he has wooden staging where
plants in pots that require sun are on the top shelf, and
those that thrive in shady humidity are on the bottom.
Different-sized coloured tiles are laid to make a Persian
carpet on the ground. Clever lighting enhances the drama
of this decorative box, even in winter, when the plants are
dormant.

Another gardener once had broad acres and grassy paths
leading to the rhododendrons and azaleas that she and
her husband loved; she moved when he died to a smaller
garden, an easily-managed sanctuary. All her expertise
has here been channelled into making a place to sit with
friends and to grow a few select and well-beloved plants; and

by constructing raised beds, she has forestalled the time when kneeling to weed or to plant bulbs finally becomes unbearable. Of course, she has no lawn. Her whole motive when she moved was to ease up on herself. Instead of grass, a paved area outside the kitchen is just large enough for a good-sized table and chairs and a long seat on which she likes to sunbathe among her white flowers.

Years ago, when we were living in Greece, we knew a couple who used to protest that they couldn't *both* come to stay with us to see the wild flowers in spring (even though we'd promised to take them to the mountains of the Epirus and to the Peloponnese) because they couldn't *both* leave the *Cytisus* × *praecox*. A procumbent broom? Goodness! They weren't abandoning an ailing parent or a child with croup, a race-horse or a three-line whip. It was the first time I was made aware of the tenacity of gardens. Today only one of those two is alive, and the broom has long since been relinquished, but the gardener does have her freedom and the place she now has is designed specifically to be periodically forsaken – though Michael and I, alas, are no longer in a position to offer her the wild flowers of Greece.

Whether you move or whether you remain where you are, unless you adapt and make things easier, more practical and less of a drudgery for yourself, you won't avoid ending by hating the garden. This is the saddest thing of all: a place that saps your enjoyment by becoming a burden takes away every attribute that makes gardening worthwhile. Instead of it being a garden of pleasure, you end up as its prisoner.

The Merit of Mistiming

Gardens are forgiving. When I've neglected mine for a month in autumn as I try to finish a book by the publisher's deadline, outside the window the place appears to have paused, waiting for me to catch up. Fortunately, when eventually I do put on my gardening clothes, I don't feel fazed by passing the bulbs in the hall still unplanted or seeing the mess of unswept leaves and the general untidiness. I know I should be tucking up the garden for winter, putting in the couple of trees still in their containers outside the back door, and pruning some of the roses. But unless the winter is early and relentlessly awful, everything I've postponed can be done at another time from when it was intended.

A gardener with whom I was discussing the breaking of rules told me of his unorthodox methods. According to the horticultural establishment, trees should be transplanted only when the sap is down. 'It's an accepted dictum, isn't it?' He then told me how he moved a twelve-foot crab apple in July. 'I knew the hole should've been prepared and that compost and all that stuff should've gone in but, you know, I hadn't the time. I was in a hurry and needed the space for a gothic folly.' With reckless bravado and enormous confidence he dug up the tree, put it into the un-nourished hole, poured a bucket of water over it, and hoped for the best. 'You know, it didn't even turn a leaf.' But if this sounds cavalier treatment of a malus just after flowering, his next anecdote sounded like murder. An acer, more than twenty feet high, was growing exactly where he wanted to build a dark-room. 'There wasn't an alternative, you see. The tree had to go. I got an axe and slashed the roots until I could haul the tree onto its side, but I still couldn't free the brute. Its tap root was impossible to get up single-handed.' Having no chance of help until the following weekend, he propped the tree upright again and stamped back the earth. 'You'll never believe it, but during the week I had a brainwave. The cellar. Perfect! What a dark-room that would make.' He roared with delight at his ingenuity. 'Much better than down the garden. So I dashed out, said a little prayer to the tree' (and he put his hands together) 'apologized profusely, gave the trunk a pat, and after a massive watering, would you believe it? The tree flourished, and is now better than ever!' No grudges, no recriminations, after such headstrong treatment: the mutilations to the tree were nothing compared to its stamina.

Stories like these are the breath of life to gardeners. Or they should be, and particularly to those who feel they are either stranded or going down for the third time. The horrible things I've done in this garden are shame-making, yet against all the rules things have survived. On the other hand, where I've lavished cherishing concern – shading an ailing tree with an umbrella in an over-scorching summer, or copiously feeding a *Drimys winteri* as it sickened before my eyes – no amount of devotion has stopped their decline. I knew a French gardener who dug up anything sickly and put it in her *hôpital*. This was an area of protected and well-nourished ground where she kept things for sometimes as long as two years while she nursed them back to health before returning them to the garden. A garden hospital? It's an idea.

The Benison of Pottering

Pottering is something I could never have done when Michael and I were gardening. Whenever we were outside our minds were set on the task in hand; pottering wasn't even a word in our vocabulary. Anyway, I don't think you can potter with someone else; it's essentially a solitary occupation, with your thoughts and body flaccid, receptive, pleasantly limp and, above all, without an iota of purpose in what you are about. Even the word emits a sense of relaxation, of desultory drifting in contrast, say, to lounging.

'To potter' is a verb without a single negative attribute. It requires no justification. No one can ever be held in disapprobation for doing it, nor reproached by an assiduous gardener – the pastime is far too valid – but you may be accused of wasting time. You and I know it isn't: the utter uselessness of such a dilatory activity makes it invaluable. Pottering is a misunderstood minor art, generating its own unique form of lonely well-being.

In the maelstrom of youth I never had the time to potter. Come to think of it, there's a watershed in one's life – late, or later on – when pottering first takes off. Now, in my back garden, it's one of life's sweeteners. Obligatory pottering belongs to this way of gardening and it's something to be undertaken at any time of day, on any occasion when I open the door and, without any purpose, walk outside. Fiddling with this or that, hovering around the Cat House, pinching a leaf, shifting a pot, tinkering with stones, trifling with bits of ivy – pausing as I go – has a recuperative quality hard to find in other occupations. How easy to become adept enough to qualify as a professional potterer.

Besides pottering, there is the pleasure of being on the inside looking out. I don't mean merely in the abstract, but physically, when standing idly by a window. This is a refinement of garden enjoyment that should never be underestimated. We may not be able to do it as often as we'd like when we're at home, but the pleasure to be found in being asked into other gardeners' houses is infallible. There's a garden near here where, on my first visit, I marvelled at the pictorial effect of seeing trees beyond trees outside the drawing-room window. It reminded me of the Burrell Collection near Glasgow where, because walls of glass have been used for the building, the woods, the bracken, the bluebells are an integral part of the gallery spaces. This being on the inside looking out is in itself one of the major exhibits – and then you turn round towards the Collection proper to see the magnificent tapestries, protected from sunlight by the grove of chestnut trees looming beyond the glass.

Random Thoughts on Writing

I know of only one person who is able to work outside on academic pursuits while around her the garden goes to pot. I admire her. It requires a great single-mindedness and an iron resolution to turn a blind eye and maintain one's concentration, I can't do it. Inside, yes, but if I try to write outside (other than putting down scribbled thoughts), I'm too easily distracted by a million other ideas that come floating through the ether.

Writing on a machine rather than throwing away draft after draft of altered text may save the South American rainforest, but when nine pages disappeared through a moment's carelessness at the end of one afternoon, a kind of frenzied insanity overwhelmed me as I pushed every possible key in an effort to recover what I'd lost. Before my eyes nine pages vanished as I passively watched, thinking they were being copied – material gathered from handfuls of little scrappy notes I'd written to myself over months of briefly sitting in the garden or in quite uncon-nected surroundings. I felt sick when I realized it was gone forever. I couldn't remember a single word or thought. If it had been nine pages about French gardeners or chefs, I would at least have had them all in notebooks taken at the actual time I was researching. Rewriting would have been a bore, yet possible. But random thoughts gathered over a year were nowhere because long ago, once they'd been transferred to the machine, I'd thrown away those scraps.

Lucky, lucky sculptor. If he or she inadvertently knocks the nose off a half-finished clay head, the organ can be modelled again. But words escape. And lost pages of a musical score must be as devastating to a composer in the middle of a composition.

Where I write I face a wall, a white wall with nothing on it but one large wood engraving by Gertrude Hermes, entitled *More People*, of naked figures, statuesque and strong, against a background of gulls and distant waves. When I'm stuck for words, the static, never-changing scene, nothing to do with horticulture, doesn't automatically induce wool-gathering. Rather, I find that following with my eye the engraver's powerful line joining one figure to another induces a tranquil state in which something provocative and totally unrelated might, just might, enter my head.

Would what one writes be quite different, according to one's surroundings?

What if the picture in front of me were a Camille Pissarro? Would writing facing Piero della Francesca's calm and sheltering *Madonna of Mercy* in the polyptych at San Sepolcro result in words being serenely placed under the beneficence of her gaze? Would prose written in a garden rise from a different source from that written in a train, or at a café table? And music? How would our sentences lie on the page if instead of Gregorian chant we wrote to Janáček or Jelly Roll Morton? Carry the idea further – would we stride like a Titan about our gardens to Mahler, or sway to the last movement in Sibelius's Fifth

Symphony as the music plies like a shuttle on a loom
between great swoops of the warp? Oscillating to that sound
while weeding, we might find we'd thrown everything away
including the trowel. Against a background of harpsichord
music, how patiently we could unpick the strands of a
clematis clinging to the wrong thing. And harpsichords,
all that family, would be ideal instruments to accompany
the finicky job of pricking-out. If each of us was set down
to make our first garden to the sound of universal music,
would we all come up with the same design? I hope not.

I long to be taken seriously when I say that I am not
a serious gardener. But because I write books, people
assume too much. They think I'm an expert. Those who
don't know me say: 'You protest too much.' Those who
know me accept my limitations. They are my closest friends.
David Wheeler, the editor of *Hortus*, is one; he lets me
write about the other end of gardening – far from history,
propagation and hormone rooting-powder. Another friend
is Katharine Swift. She has opened many doors for me into
the gardening world, not least by giving me a translation
of a Dutch saying: 'The sweetness of country life goes
well with books.' The thought couldn't be more apt for
her. Researching into primary sources at the Bodleian
Library, at Morville Hall near Bridgnorth in Shropshire
she's made a series of unique gardens which reflect horticulture through the centuries. Her many designs, including an apothecary's, Tudor, sixteenth- and seventeenth-
century, a knot and a kitchen garden, are separated by
grass paths. On one side is a long and deep bed filled
with flowers beloved by the Victorians, including dozens of

superb shrub and climbing roses – a lusciously overwhelming sight in summer.

Katharine accepts my attitude to gardening, and rather than chide me for protesting my ignorance, she does her best to enlighten me. We know each other so well that when she describes a plant she thinks I might like, she doesn't wait for me to ask, but tells me to what family it belongs and, more practically, how to spell it. In other words, she accepts my botanical deficiency, since it in no way impedes our shared enjoyment of gardens, books and everything to do with the subject; we don't have to play games with one another. In true friendship, we make a space for each other and keep it available regardless of politics, religion, academic credentials, or the way we choose to fritter bits of life away. She writes from her head, I write from the neck down, but when we talk our conversation weaves to and fro between the two dominions of academia and childhood sighs over Matthew Arnold's *The Forsaken Merman*. She loves a day spent in bed. I've tried, but much as the idea of getting up late appeals to me, I never, never can. It's hopeless; against my will I'm forced to start living early in the morning – even in the winter, when most creatures have a natural predisposition to hibernation – but Katharine can write in bed, read there (of course), and spend the whole day in relaxed enjoyment of the 'sweetness of country life' among books and cats, while I remain hopping mad with envy.

When I began writing, one of my first assignments was an article on Rosemary Verey and her garden for an up-market American magazine. (This was years ago, when she was still living in the main house.) Nervously I arrived at Barnsley House, and admitted that though I had meagre horticultural knowledge, I did like looking at gardens even if I couldn't put a name to what I was seeing. Rosemary was kind and patient, encouraged me to keep going. Each time I returned, to see her garden at different seasons, she answered my questions however puerile they were. I haven't forgotten, Rosemary: at our first encounter you set a precedent for the kindness of gardeners (they're far more generous than cooks) that hasn't been eroded since.

The reality is that when I write I have to check everything, or try to. It's not enough for me to say 'that nice blue thing', which is what mentally I'm doing. In my mind I'm blundering about for the word, for a name, for an approximation of what I'm meaning. In conversation it's all right to say, 'Oh, *you* know – that wonderful spire called . . . or something like that?' Then, whoever I'm with usually catches on and proclaims the right name. It's the same walking round my garden, as anyone will know who comes here. We stand in front of something: I'm asked the name: I grope, I can't remember: if they are serious, and really don't know either, I then resort to my Idiot Book, in which I've written down the name and position of each salient plant I've brought into the garden. But even this scheme falls apart when I move things – which I'm constantly doing – and then forget to write down where I've put them.

Facts may elude me, but hare-brained schemes are something else, and until a friend's eyes glaze over I enjoy taking off into cloud-cuckoo-land. That's why Richard Craven (who has done a lot of work for me in the garden: the archway, the path, the Cat House and so on) and I get on so well. It's intoxicating when you find someone who fizzes with the same exuberance. An idea, frail and shadowy, fills up the space in a second as we urge each other on with this or that embellishment to some imagined structure. We may scrap the lot and start again, but out of discarded projects slowly comes some design that pleases us. As I'm innumerate I can never answer questions about how wide or high I want something. I hate the practicalities and have to depend on my eyes, but Richard will come up with factual suggestions. The roof of the Cat House should be so wide, so deep, and he draws his idea on paper and then, while my mind is still messing with shingles or tiles, he'll say, 'The roof *must* be made of copper! Curved, of course.' Then I protest that it'll look too stark – I want ribs running the width, to break up the line; Richard has more sense than to ask me how many ribs, but immediately catches on to the suggestion, and together we discuss how the ends of the ribs will be finished off, for the look of the building head-on.

If ever I have my vaulted wooden bridge spanning the garden, with a seat on top for a bird's-eye view, Richard will be the person I will go to without hesitation, knowing with absolute confidence that he'll pick up on what I'm getting at. At present he's working on a magnificent pagoda for a gardener in the Chilterns. It's his own vision of *chinoiserie*, made of chestnut and with such movement and flow to the wood that looking up from the inside you feel faint with the knowledge that this is perfection.

Deliverance from Bondage

A 'low maintenance' garden is a phrase I dislike. We know
what it implies: a series of so many compromises that your
heart isn't in it, and you might just as well have a window
box. But for those overwhelmed by the upkeep of a garden
they've been left with, the phrase holds out promises: it
offers solutions, escape and, above all, a hope of shedding
guilt. Hence the sad figures cruising round the gardening
shelves on wet afternoons. Unable to be of much practical
use, I can at least write about the things that have made life
easier for me since I've been coping on my own.

At the risk of being a bore, I must reiterate that one of
the greatest of garden tyrants, more than pruning, watering, digging or manuring, is *the lawn*. Ask gardeners, and
they admit that mowing is a chore. It's one never-ending
torment, and yet they are compelled to do it. According to a
recent survey, eighty-eight per cent of gardens have a lawn,
despite the fact that, after weeding, mowing comes top of
the list of the most-hated jobs. Worse yet: it was stated in the
press recently – a quite sickening fact – that the 'average'
gardener spends more than half his time (and usually it
is his, not hers) working on the lawn. Half his time? Think
of it! All those hours thrown away on maintenance, to the
detriment of creativity. Years ago David Hicks in his book
Garden Design – full of good ideas that are still applicable
today – recommended doing away with lawns in small

gardens. He considered them unnecessary to the overall design, and only a trouble to look after.

Unfortunately, years of being brain-washed into thinking that gardens must revolve round lawns has meant that too many people have been conditioned for far too long for them to be able to accept his dictum. The greenness of sward, bare feet on grass, a place where children can sprawl, are essential parts of summer. We dream of languishing through hot afternoons on lawns as sensuous as velvet; of lying in dappled light with limbs spread, as relaxed as a cat, and feeling beneath our fingers turf as springy as a ripe Camembert.

Ah, those dreams. In classic settings, lawns are perfection: they are grand, generous, cohesive and magnificent – but you and I, with our small plots, and as the sole gardener, why should we feel persecuted? Why are there constantly questions on the air and columns in the press about how to keep the lawn in faultless condition? Life is real, life is earnest, and now, particularly in view of the desperate straits of gardeners having to cope with water shortages, isn't it worth considering countries where there's no rainfall for months, yet their flowering shrubs and trees are superb even without a lawn to set them off? Why on earth do the British continue to be so obsessed with lawns?

Imagine the bliss of life without a mower. Unburdened, my relationship with this garden became a two-way love affair. It was as though I'd shed a load – a burden that for a year had kept me apprehensive, dreading to look out of the window after a gentle fall of rain to see how much grass had grown and, while drinking coffee at breakfast, have to face the question: to mow, or not to mow? Once I'd stopped being bullied by machinery, I wondered how I could have misused so much effort over yards of cable, fids of grass choking the blades, the hazard of concealed pebbles, and all the clearing up afterwards, when other things in the garden give me so much pleasure. Weeding, for instance. I'm saddened that weeding comes top of the most-hated jobs since I find it a passive and constructive pastime, in the same way that some people find ironing calming. The result of weeding is rewarding; I can't say that with confidence about my ironing.

Anyone with a small garden, coping alone, should from the first rid themselves of tyranny. All that's needed is courage, followed by alternatives. Freedom from lawns generates endless ingenious ideas: you could lay down gravel or paving; slate, bricks, or mixtures of other things. There are all sorts of materials, varying in size and colour, ready to use, that work well with plants. In my case, as I was limited by having access only through the house, I chose bark chippings, easy to handle and distribute. I had no idea how it would work – either aesthetically or practically – but after several years' experience of it I would use bark again. One immediate advantage is that it requires neither feeding nor scarifying; bulbs come up through the loose bits without the bother of keeping grass under control; and best of all for an untidy gardener like myself, when things like the willow trees and box need clipping I don't have to gather up the bits because a quick raking-over conceals the lot amid the chippings. It's also walkable-on at any time of the year; there's no need to change your shoes when in wet weather you want to make a quick foray into the garden to pick a bay leaf or rescue a drooping plant.

I hardly grow any flowers; in fact, I've today decided to get rid of the Japanese anemones engulfing more space than I allotted them. I know how biddable they are in certain ways – they'll grow in impoverished soil, in semi-shade, in orchard turf – but here they've become so dense that anything malignant like bindweed or ground elder is impossible to eradicate from among the clumps. Lovely as they are with tall stems that don't need staking, and their delicate cups of white with yellow stamens, or the ones the colour of mulberries or dusty flesh, in the restricted space I have they mean continual confrontation. Instead, would I be better with sedums, the tall autumnal ones, *S. spectabile*, that bring butterflies floating over the wall? I like them for their gritty-textured heads and uncompromising grossness. I'll wait before deciding.

The great comfort in doing something so ruthless as eviction comes from knowing I can give the anemones to Tamsin for her country garden. For what gardener can throw away a plant? Or dig up an unwanted shrub without first knowing there's a welcoming home somewhere? Last year, appalled at the ugliness of a bottle-brush tree I'd bought on impulse for its grey-green leaves, I was eternally grateful to a neighbour who opened his arms to it. This year he is so pleased with this antipodean reject. The bright red spikes suit his garden admirably, whereas in mine, beside a coppery pittosporum, they looked monstrous. Now I'm dithering over my *Solanum crispum*. Another summer has passed in cowardice as I hesitate to pass judgement on a climber with the generous habit of flowering for months on end. Shall I be intrepid and banish it? For one thing, I don't like its smell of rancid dog biscuits; but it's also too rampant for the corner where I have it, thrusting out green arms in all directions. The shrub never becomes exhausted, but I do. The more I cut it back, the more it thrives, until now I'm slashing away at four-foot wands still covered with clusters of buds promising a floriferous and doggy autumn. How churlish to complain – and yet, do I want the solanum appropriating a precious corner, just for the sake of its blue flowers with orange centres exactly echoing the colour of a *Lonicera* × *tellmanniana* which tangles through it? I didn't know I'd get this effect, I can't take credit for having planned the colours this way – it happened inadvertently – but there's pleasure to be had every time I walk past the performing duo. And anyway, with what would I replace the solanum? A delightful dilemma – an opportunity to vacillate while doing nothing dramatic.

Indecisions, indecisions. The instability of wavering is a pleasant contrast to having to buy one's daily bread.

Clematis Have a Way with Them

At the moment I've gone soft over clematis. The whole family of them. This is partly because I don't have many flowers here, but primarily because their versatility puts them into a class of their own. Clematis are perfect for a small garden, and now that Treasures of Tenbury, on my doorstep, are once more in the ascendancy with their clematis nursery, the possibilities are countless. Where rose climbers and ramblers cry for space, clematis find their own terrain; they move among the shrubs and trees with such sinuous grace that you might have thought my garden was their natural habitat. And unlike my old-fashioned roses, they span the year: there's a clematis for almost every season, starting with *C. armandii* which I love for its scent and felty flowers, arriving as it does so early in the year. There are other even earlier clematis. One, the angelic nodding *C. cirrhosa balearica* with freckled creamy bells that I've seen growing in Hampshire, hasn't a chance here. But what does it matter? There are so many others to go for. Only the real gardeners of this world lament what they can't have. Just as real gardeners want Shangri-La flowers with perpetual youth.

One of the advantages of being reckless was unexpected: having filled this garden with trees, I now find that I've numerous branched hosts for clematis to insinuate, drape or twine themselves around. Up among the topmost limbs of my young amelanchier is 'Henryi', whose large white flowers have almost a look of Nancy Reagan's stare, gazing artlessly at the President. Certainly their size and expression are in stark contrast to the little white flowers of the snowy mespilus that appear much earlier in the year, before the tree has leaves.

Planted at the foot of my recently freed-from-bondage quince tree is 'Etoile Violette', one of my favourite long-lasting viticellas. Another is the lush and deeply purple 'Royal Velour', a compliant and late-summer flowering clematis that integrates almost anywhere in the garden, unlike the brazen, jumbo-sized ones I regard as far more difficult to place – if at all. There is one, though, 'Comtesse de Bouchaud', that I love for her extravagantly free-flowering amplitude and the way she scrambles into the *Buddleja alternifolia* after the buddleja's flowers are over.

Sometimes I try deliberately to change the character of the host tree by using a clematis that contrasts with the earlier flowers. My Bramley apple tree, loaded with blossom in spring, later turns into a pink parasol from 'Hagley Hybrid' festooning its spread branches. From being a rustic tree belonging to pastoral orchards, by late summer the delicacy of the clematis has turned it into something urbane and surprising to find at the end of the garden alongside the wheelbarrow and compost bins.

I've also tried doing the reverse. If you plant a *C. flammula* at the foot of an early-flowering crab apple, *Malus floribunda*, you get a second helping of white blossom when the clematis covers the tree with its myriad tiny white flowers smelling so much of hawthorn that the sight and scent resurrect spring. Actually, I think I could be more adventurous with this clematis. How would it look, I wonder, against the shiny wetness of the immense holly tree growing at the end of the garden?

Long ago I lost my heart to *Clematis chrysochoma*, though I don't see it often in gardens. With small, dusty pink flowers in early summer and downy leaves, it's ideal as groundcover or else twining alone over a wooden pergola where nothing can confuse its modest poise.

Other clematis are into other trees: 'Pink Fantasy' is slowly and prettily twining into the *Prunus* × *subhirtella* 'Autumnalis'; 'Mrs Cholmondeley' with her blowzy huge blue flowers will follow after the yellow tassels of *Laburnum* × *watereri* 'Vossii'; 'Royal Velour' is softening the tortured stance of my wisteria tree.

Something that doesn't have a high profile among the gardening establishment is the deciduous sweet pepper bush, *Clethra alnifolia*, that has creamy scented racemes of flower in late summer. I can't say it's a knock-out, but it does have its moments. The tree reaches about six feet when fully grown, and though not reliably robust in cold areas, survived the prolonged east wind of last winter when the rosemary, teucriums and sages succumbed. As so often happens with plants, things you take on half-heartedly grow on you. And this tree has, on me. In late summer the clethra is a vision of naturally-evolved artistry: the tulip-shaped, deep pink flowers of a *Clematis texensis* 'Duchess of Albany' have escaped from the trellis and festoon the tree with decorative scrolling, something I had never envisaged but which, now that it has happened, pleases me with its vagrancy.

Clematis do have two indisputable drawbacks – but then, what or who hasn't at least one? Two flies-in-the-ointment are hardly life-threatening. Humans are far worse.

Pruning them is what fazes most gardeners. But as long as you know the name of your plant, a good clematis book will tell you exactly which of three categories its pruning comes into: tidying-up after flowering (early things like alpinas); light pruning in February or March (the summer clematis); or hard pruning in February or March (the later-flowering types). Beside each clematis in my Idiot Book I write in red the figure 1, 2 or 3 to remind me when each one should be pruned. Brilliant – an infallible system. Well, it should be; but sometimes, as with even the best plans in life, things become muddled, either on the paper or in the bed, and when I'm out there with the secateurs and can't recognize where the thing begins or ends, I often bungle the procedure. But I'll tell you something from experience – having made the error so often: if you prune at the wrong season you don't kill the plant, all it means is that the poor thing is thwarted of its natural timing and flowers out of step. Given a pruning in spring, an early clematis will obligingly flower in summer, and those I completely neglected to prune in spring will cover the place with flowers long before their time.

Here then is hope for both the novice gardener and the one with creaking joints. Keep your cool, don't flap, and remember how intrinsic to a garden is the forgivingness of plants. It's a quality to be revered.

Wilt is something else. When you're faced with your first attack of wilt, it's the end of the world. Or so it seems. When Michael and I planted the first three clematis we ever bought – 'Duchess of Edinburgh', 'Mrs Cholmondeley' and a *tangutica*, and the duchess got the wilt, distraught with anxiety I rang Treasures, from where we'd bought them. What was this little damp drooping thing with limp leaves? Where had I gone wrong? Was the plant doomed? The professional voice down the phone reassured me that I needn't worry. Wilt is a common clematis malady, and not necessarily fatal: all I need do was follow the ailing strand to the ground, and cut it off. Since then I've never looked back: wilt is a bore, but there's no need to panic. And I've found clematis extremely resilient when I've treated them shabbily and overlooked watering them sufficiently. The plant may punish me by sulking for a season, but the next year, grubbing about in the earth, I find miraculous and fragile green shoots about to leap into space with a life-force that quite restores my loyalty to gardens. Lovely, lovely plant, come back, do, and I promise to water you copiously.

Next year's list of clematis and where I think I'll grow them is already bounding across my 'Forward Planning' page of garden imperatives. We write ourselves memos of jobs to be done that are never all crossed off; they carry on from one week to another, from month to month, sometimes from year to year. It's a part of gardening as commonplace as using the boot scraper. Sometimes the only alteration to the columns under Spring and Autumn is a change of year at the top of the page.

Ignorant gardeners are warned against buying plants unless they know where they are going to put them. Such sound and utterly irrefutable advice. And how boring. Anyway, who takes it? Really, who does? Who hasn't at some time or other seen an irresistible thing in a nursery, or been offered a treasure by a friend, and then returned home stumped? Where on earth shall I put it? But does it matter? The whole gardening edifice won't come tumbling down about one's ears. At worst you have to move it several times – or, as I had to do with the bottle-brush tree, you give it away.

If you are simplifying life in the garden, as I am, what more can you want than clematis, clematis and more clematis? They are sweet, thornless, embellishing, versatile, and their variety of flowers can dress a garden in whatever form you choose, from the demurely latent to the brazenly vulgar. Although, as with roses, you aren't filling the place with scents, you are working with one of the most agreeable families, moreover one that adds to the horizontal planes of the garden with prostrate travellers, or the vertical elevations with lightweight scramblers. Supine or upright, they are a gift to people like you and me, left to deal with a garden single-handed.

I've gone on about clematis in this way because I do know they're something that might be of use to anyone faced with a too-demanding type of garden. Ease up on yourself; cut down the number of plants you grow, with their differing demands, and go for things of an agreeable disposition. You won't be down-grading the garden in any way, merely moving into a different pattern of gardening. No lawn; lots of trees with lots of clematis growing up them, is a fairly basic recipe. But it doesn't put an end to all those decorative and fiddly bits of planting that are so enjoyable, and can be used like colourful punctuation marks, telling you when to breathe.

Some Positive Thoughts

Gardens take shape much faster than you think. I couldn't believe, once the hard designs were laid, how quickly things sprang into being. By the second year the leaves on the outstretched branches of the lime trees, although not yet touching, already gave the garden height and linear strength.

Frost, which I hadn't expected in a walled garden, had

me almost in tears when I saw what it had done to the juvenile ceanothus, but behold! behind the crispy buds others emerged later. Every year the ceanothus has flowered prodigiously, from the most awful hole under a drystone wall.

If you're left with a garden that's increasingly too much to cope with, fence off all but the bit near to the house. Fill the banished area with shrubs that will eventually grow into integrating mounds close enough together to smother the weeds. Weeds. I have a lot of nice things to say about them. Not only do I enjoy weeding, but I refuse to feel threatened by many of them because I'm dead set on enjoying this garden, my last, rather than behaving like a disciplinary nanny. So the lovely bright and varnished celandines with glossy leaves rise from the bark in spring to spread across the brown pelt in a huge Croesus carpet, only to sink into the underworld again leaving not a trace of their existence. Herb Robert is another invader that softens the base of walls with its grace and lacy foliage. But rosebay willowherb (I loved the tall pink group against my fence the first year here) has had to be expelled. The seeds impregnated the garden from one end to the other so effectively that by the end of winter its fat green progeny littered the place (shallow-rooted, they have the advantage of being easily removed).

In the way of gardens, things can work well for you unintentionally. In late summer and quite fortuitously, a brash and showy magenta clematis with large flowers, 'Ernest Markham', has clambered into the burnished bronze leaves of a pittosporum standing against the wall. More impressively, its wayfaring behaviour has thrust it into the branches of a clerodendron, a quite startling small tree with white

flowers surrounded by maroon calyces that are later transformed into brilliant blue berries. The combination of the
pittosporum, the clematis and the clerodendron is idyllic.
At their feet and quite by chance a lacecap hydrangea (one
of the sublime designs of garden shrubs, with flat corymbs
ringed by petals) flowers at the same time. Because the
hydrangea is pink though it's meant to be blue, the colour
couldn't be better placed as clerodendron, clematis and
shrubs all appear together at the end of summer. I didn't
know this would happen so I can't take credit for having
planned it this way – but it's a great thing to discover
you've been unwittingly skilful, and the pleasure I get from
walking up and down past this performing quartet is an
unalloyed bonus. No wonder visitors have been impressed
by my acumen. Only I know it was luck, not sagacity: I
couldn't pretend that it was otherwise. But this is the
thrust of gardening; this is what urges us on to continually
pull ourselves out of one trough, before tumbling down
the other side into a succeeding chasm. The rhythmic
motion of disaster followed by success sustains a belief in
the ultimate magnanimity of gardens.

An Easeful Approach to Autumn

Autumn is the time of year when the garden moves into
my own personal space. I don't mean physically, but that,
after the quiet lull that comes at the end of summer, the
garden once again encroaches on my thoughts, sapping

me of frivolous conjectures based on nothing but fantasy. When I discovered in October that a vigorous honeysuckle, *Lonicera periclymenum* 'Belgica' – which earlier in the year had been flowering along the wall – had climbed into the summit of the thirty-foot fastigiate mountain ash, making a quite unexpected column of flowers, I felt I was being got at in a gentle way.

Elsewhere, through ignorance and by sheer luck – I had not weeded a sprinkling of self-seeded poppies – and by a fluke something eyecatching had taken place: a *Rosa moyesii* 'Geranium', its spreading branches covered with pendules of orange heps, had made a dramatic feature with scarlet poppies in the foreground clashing horribly. The spectacle was all due to idleness.

Of course, often the reverse happens. It isn't serendipity the whole time, far from it. When I put up two wooden arches at the end of the garden, I didn't realize until too late that it would have been wiser to plant the same roses on each side. Having a mass of the same thing gives a generous effect, and uniform foliage also visually stabilizes the arches. Honeysuckle on one side and a rose on the other left the structure lopsided. Next year another 'Alchemist' will go in, and I'll give the honeysuckle to Tamsin, who has room to absorb any number of homeless climbers.

Wandering out of the house at the end of summer, past the vulgar and flouncy pink pelargoniums that have been flowering for months and the rose 'Blushing Lucy', I enter a green garden. With the exception of various late-flowering clematis, the place is serenely unadventurous. It has an uncompetitive air, from leaf beyond leaf. Sitting on the hidden seat at the far end of the garden I can be at ease, knowing that I'm missing nothing. I like it. Only the huge flowerless wands on some vigorous climbing roses demand attention. But not today; maybe tomorrow, or at least before autumnal gales tear them off the walls and trellis.

Apart from those fronds pricking my conscience to do something about them, I ignore the words 'Tidying Up the Garden before Winter', with their nauseatingly prissy undertone. My ears are covered. I know that's what we should be doing in autumn: we should be clearing up the garden and leaving it ship-shape, with as much efficiency as some people clean the house, or their motor cars on Sunday. 'Do it before winter', we are cautioned. But in the country we never did. The frost was savage and prolonged; things did better protected under their own detritus. Only in late March or April did we really begin to clear up the remains of summer.

A top-class gardener throws us not just crumbs of comfort but great slabs of reassurance when she admits to wanting to know how a plant will die before she allows it in the garden. She demands copper leaves, sculptured seed heads, filigree outlines, skeletons, and a visual cacophony of brilliant pods, so that what pleases her in death remains as a legacy of summer. By disregarding every tenet of garden decorum, she has had the gumption to go for what she wanted: no question of 'putting the garden to bed' for her.

Here, with my ideals turned towards easeful living, there's a kinder climate and I somehow find I don't bother until spring. And then it's too late to be a serious undertaking. Anyone can change their attitude of mind; if, gazing out of the window in November, you think the place looks a shambles, comfort yourself with the knowledge that those untidy seedheads will look unbelievably miraculous outlined in rime. The sedums, lady's-mantle, rose heps, twigs, stalks and stems – all the shabby leaves and the skeletons of radiant blooms left over from last summer – when outlined in frost will transform your habitual setting into somewhere unfamiliar. You will feel you have never walked there before. Why not try it? Don't conform to this tidying-up business, but move into the territory of slothfulness. Inertia and a laid-back philosophy do have their moments. And this is one of them. From a home for shamefully neglected debris your garden will one day in winter be turned into a place of beauty, a place that is denied your neighbour, with his clean earth full of clumps of shorn stubble.

The Onset of Winter

Gardeners find it difficult not to become soppy over robins. Companionable in autumn when other birds have retired, they're almost a garden fixture. Their relationship to us is endearing and inquisitive, but among themselves they're far from benevolent. Aggressively territorial, robins display a distinctly bossy stance when a rival encroaches on their patch.

On a still day in autumn, within a few minutes of my taking up a spade, one appears. Bobbing about, the robin watches me working with eyes as shiny black as the hat-pins my grandmother used to fasten her veil. Cocking his head and unperturbed, he hovers nearby as I start clearing up my implements. Staying close he follows me about the garden and then, as I shake off my gumboots, he perches on a bench in the courtyard, waiting for me to go indoors before he searches for worms in the place where I've just lifted a pot to bring into the house. The relationship of gardener and robin is private. Nothing dramatic takes place, it's just a trust we have in each other as we move noiselessly to and fro, both assuming that the terrain belongs to us. A gardener's spontaneous response to this small creature may appear asinine – that foolish smile on finding the bird perched beside us, presaging the arrival of winter – but I can't bear to think of our loss if robins were to become rare and disappear, in the same way as wrens have from gardens, and larks from the hills.

The prospect of winter charms me. I know it means giving up a lot of things; things that are earthy and full of sensuous pleasures, such as basking, smelling lavender, and sitting amid a drone of bees. And in this town it also means not waking early to the stertorous gasp of dragons' breath from hot-air balloons rising above the Castle keep as they float towards the Welsh Marches. But winter brings with it a certain sort of jubilation, personal and not shared with many: the hope that for weeks I needn't talk about gardening.

The world is full of people talking 'shop'. At one time in our lives, when Michael and I moved among linguists and actors, we'd often be drawn into their semantic quagmires. Amusing as it was for a time to concentrate on glottal stops – interesting, even – we longed for a change of lingo, to wake up among, say, bookbinders, or topographers, had we known any. But gardeners? All I know is that by winter I want to walk away, shutting the gate behind me. Come: let's talk of Robert Browning; of travel, high passes and nomads; let's argue over fossils and arrow-heads, and wonder as the trees are shedding their last leaves why it is that lorries seem to shed their loads all the year. I yearn to talk about asteroids, footprints in the snow, films, manhole covers – and, at any time of the day, about food.

Perhaps it's a matter of prospect rather than aspect. All the summer has been engrossed with aspects one way or another; either with my own or with other people's. But prospect – there's a word trembling with potential – and never more so than when the nights close in.

Walking into the garden after working indoors for weeks, I feel no sense of reproach from the trees and shrubs I've left untended for so long. Unswept leaves have gathered into squashy flotsam, climbers have come adrift, and little seedlings have sprung up between the bricks, turning the courtyard into a miniature paddock. One gardener – who yearly intends to be in control of the situation – admits that she never manages to get her bulbs in until a mild day in January. Yet their performance is always brilliant.

This unprincipled advice is quisling talk; and some gardeners find it physically impossible to follow. Yet leisure isn't a discreditable concept when applied to the garden. If you can change your state of mind and overlook the quiet chaos falling all around you, you'll find yourself lavished with compensations. The garden carries you onto another plane. For one thing, a curious peace of mind takes over; and for another, submitting yourself to autumn allows for sanguine thoughts, thoughts that, far from galvanizing you into action, can quietly lead you into an inner world of rumination and unconscious creativity. That's a side of gardening seldom voiced.

Now more than ever, coping with a garden at the end of your life, is the time to try out this subterfuge. It's hard to anticipate with any degree of realism the revivifying effect to be had from sitting in the garden. Each time I do, I'm taken by surprise. It starts from listening to what surrounds me, rather than looking, and this is never to the forefront of a gardener's mind. My unseeing eye may fasten on something, but instead of getting up to tie it back, or fetch a nail, or pull it out, I let it wash over me as, in a state of mental vacancy, thoughts I thought I'd never think rise to the surface.

Although I no longer live where Michael and I first gardened, I can still re-create in my mind's eye the wan light of early spring mornings when the moment seemed poised and flowers were folded in repose. Surrounded by the urgency of birds, we left footprints in the dew: a fraction later and rays of the rising sun would slant across the land, changing the tempo, changing the light, before a dramatic metamorphosis took place.

There's nothing welcome about the dramatic metamorphosis that is forced on you when you are left alone with a garden at the end of your life. What happens is internal. What you make of this change – both the condition and the emotion – is up to you. For it's now that the spiritual growth of the place takes ascendancy over its physical growth. Whether the garden is being transformed before your eyes, or whether it lies in a state of suspension, the quintessence of a garden is carried within yourself. This essential quality is not easily shaken off, nor does its beneficence decline with age: it keeps in step with us, even though at times it moves unevenly. Some days our spirits are invigorated almost palpably; at other times there's a return to dull inertia. But the essential part is there, somewhere, as a bottomless source of nourishment, refreshing as travel, yet less expensive, and often rekindling your well-being when you least expect it.

I don't understand this aspect of gardening, one that has always plagued me with unanswered conjectures. All I know is that, although I'm not an acquiescent person with a fatalistic outlook who accepts my 'lot' but a fighter for the things I most care about, the garden never stops confounding me. On occasions when I've stopped struggling and gone to sit outside, the place generates such inexplicable spiritual arousal that I look round to see from where the impulse can be coming.

Some people know. The answer is a certainty: the vigour comes from their religion, of whatever denomination. But for me that is no answer, because I wouldn't know where to place the question. 'What is essential is invisible to the eye,' said the Little Prince, thinking of his sheep and flower alone on their planet, in Antoine de Saint-Exupéry's allegorical tale. Yes. Of course, and how comforting. 'What is essential is invisible to the eye' applies to my garden. Without fudging reality, the contemplation of space and time becomes a solace, and all our human endeavours are put into perspective.

Immortality – whether for a garden or ourselves – is a self-centred concept. How restful then to consider our brevity against aeons of Aboriginal 'dream time' through the breadth of evolving geology or species, or the grains of sand on ocean shores. And if for a while some of us have made nothing more than what Derek Jarman described as 'a little wilderness at the heart of paradise', what more is needed? As we move from light to dark towards infinity, how can any of us standing in our gardens be anything but vanishing motes in the unfathomable vastness of eternity?

Some of the Books, People and Places
Referred to in the Text

Alexander, C., *A Pattern of Language*, O.U.P. 1977
Christopher, Thomas, *In Search of Lost Roses*, Bloomsbury 1996
Derek Jarman's Garden with photographs by Howard Sooley, Thames & Hudson 1995
Dutton, G.F. *Harvesting the Edge*, Menard Press 1995
Fearnley-Whittingstall, Jane, *Ivies*, Chatto & Windus 1992
Hortus, A Gardening Journal (Proprietor David Wheeler), Bryan's Ground, Stapleton, nr Presteigne, Herefordshire LD8 2LP
Jekyll, Gertrude, *Garden Ornament*, Antique Collectors' Club 1982
Keen, Mary, *Decorate Your Garden*, Conrad Octopus 1993
Pollan, Michael, *Second Nature*, Bloomsbury 1996
Salmon, Tim, *The Unwritten Places*, Lycabettus Press, Athens 1995
Scott-James, Anne, *Sissinghurst – The Making of a Garden*, Michael Joseph 1975
Yates, Chris, *The Secret Carp*, Merlin Unwin Books 1992

Craven, Richard, Carpenter, Church Cottage, Stoke St Milborough, Ludlow, Shropshire SY8 2EJ, Tel: 01584 823631
Finlay, Dr Ian Hamilton, Little Sparta, Dunsyre, Lanarkshire, Strathclyde, Scotland
Hicks, Ivan, Garden House, Stanstead Park, Rowlands Castle, Hants PO9 6DX, Tel: 01705 413149
Jones, Jessie, Fernleigh, St Julian's Avenue, Ludlow, Shropshire SY8 1ET
Smith, Joe, Prestige Stoneworks, Crocketford, Dumfries, Scotland, Tel: 01556 690632
Swift, Dr Katharine, The Dower House, Morville Hall Gardens, nr Bridgnorth, Shropshire WV16 5NB, Tel: 01746 714407
Whichford Pottery, nr Shipton on Stour, Warwickshire CV36 5PG, Tel: 01608 584833

INDEX

agapanthus 81, 108-9
Alexander, C.: *A Pattern of Language* 126
alpine phlox 122
apertures 49-50, 125-6
apple trees 107, 200
Arbuthnott, Louisa & James 9
artificial flowers 51, 142
asphodel 81
Australian tree fern 172
autumn 206-9

bamboo 151
bark chippings 114, 196
bay tree 43
Beefsteak plant 164
begonias 160, 162
Berberis 160
bereavement 175-9, 212
bergenia 161
bindweed 147-8
birds 61, 68-9, 87, 94, 101, 134, 135, 209-10
black flowers 168
borders 45-6
bottle-brush tree 197
box, golden 160
Breakwell, Sylvia 25-6
buddleja 41, 99, 110-12, 200
buildings 127-31, 158, 169-70
butterflies 59, 61
buying plants 39-40, 139, 203

campanula 46, 61, 123
Castle Howard 29
ceanothus 40-1, 82, 112, 205
celandine 205
cherry 154-5
children 3-4, 34, 114-15
Chilean glory flower 159
Christopher, Thomas: *In Search of Lost Roses* 91-2
cistus 43, 101
clematis 44, 69-70, 127-8, 151, 152, 164, 198-205
clerodendron 108, 205-6
coleus 151, 165
colour 10, 54, 77, 80-2, 163
conifers 158
cottage garden 58, 61, 75
courtyard 100-1
cranesbill 173
Craven, Richard 129, 192-3
crocosmia 161
cut flowers 51-2, 122
cyclamen 112, 115

dahlias 160-1
dandelion 146
death of plants 43, 208
doors 49, 100
Drimys winteri 13, 15, 185
Dungeness 27

INDEX

Dutton, G.F. 28-9

embroidery designs 152-3
eucalyptus 105-6, 115
eucryphia 109-10
evictions 197
Evison, Raymond 164
experiments 115-16

fashion 142
Fearnley-Whittingstall, J. 132
Festuca glauca 165
feverfew 75
Finlay, Ian Hamilton 29
flowers 35-6, 56-7, 74-6, 197
formal design 46-7
forsythia 155
France 21, 25, 43, 81, 103, 120, 161, 169
fruit trees 8, 53, 61, 106-7
fuchsia 167-8
furniture 99, 128, 135, 150, 163, 170

garden centres 39-40
garden rubbish 113-14
gardening books 2, 6, 55
gender 32-3, 37, 93
geranium 157, 168
gladioli 147
Goldsworthy, Andy 27
grasses 165
green garden 96, 207
Grizedale Forest 26-7, 132

Haseley Court 54, 163
heather 152
hebe 154, 157, 164
Hedera 165
hedges 45, 53, 65, 125, 160
herb Robert 205
Hicks, D.: *Garden Design* 194
Hicks, Ivan 29-32
Hidcote 125
holly, variegated 155
hollyhock 75-6
honeysuckle 45, 101, 207
hornbeam 45, 47, 53, 125
house 34, 45-6, 52
houseleek 32, 115
Hubbard, John 30
hydrangea 51, 82, 101, 206
hypericum 154

illusion 51-3, 77, 100
Inverewe 27
island beds 152-3
ivy 52, 131-3, 153, 165

jacaranda 81, 109
Japanese anemone 101, 197
Jarman, Derek 27-9, 114, 214
jasmine 42, 151
Jekyll, Gertrude 46, 150
Jones, Jessie 127

kitchen garden 61, 94, 118-21

lady's mantle 39
Lancaster, Nancy 54, 163
lavender 25, 101, 108, 123
lawns 114, 152, 194-6
leaving 85-8, 145, 179-81
Leighton, C.: *Four Hedges* 71
levels 44-5, 97
ligularia 80
lime, pleached 103-5, 204
Linaria triornithophora 164
Little Sparta 29
locality 42, 82
London 53, 56-7, 62
Lonicera 198, 207
Love-lies-bleeding 169
low maintenance garden 194-8

MacKenzie, Osgood 27
magnolia 41, 42, 110-11
mirrors 53, 133-4
Mitella breweri 157
Moghul garden 95
monkey-puzzle tree 158
mood 76-83, 160
morning glory 81, 173
moving plants 101
Munstead Wood 46

Nicolson, Harold 47
Nicotiana sylvestris 144
nurseries 40

oleander 81, 147
orchids, wild 81
origanum 155, 157
originality 25-33, 37

paint 127, 136-8, 150, 163
pansy 38-9, 122, 139, 153
passion flower 151
paths 46, 96, 99-100, 160
patio 162-4
pepper tree 172-3
photographers 16-22
pittosporum 159, 205-6
plumbago 172
poached-egg flower 154

poinsettia 164-5
Pollan, M.: *Second Nature* 138
ponds/pools 7, 66-9, 94, 151-2
poppy 4, 51, 81, 140, 207
pots 54, 116, 121-4
pottering 186-7
Powis Castle 109
primrose 62
pruning 40-1, 201-2
Prunus 155

quince 106, 199

red-hot poker 150-1
refuge 5-6, 37, 83
rhubarb 61-2
rockery 156-7
roof garden 94, 115, 142
rose 30, 42, 44, 68, 72-3, 101-2, 113, 116, 140-1, 166-9
Rose of Sharon 154
Royal Horticultural Society 13
Rubus thibetanus 103
rule-breaking 40, 44, 184-5
Russell, James 30
rust 30-2, 134-5

Sackville-West, Vita 47, 165
St John's wort 154
Salmon, Tim: *The Unwritten Places* 73-4
scents 4, 77, 113, 142-4
Scott-James, A.: *Sissinghurst* 47
sculptural gardens 26-7
scything 70-1
sedum 153, 157, 197
shelving 135
Sissinghurst 46
Smith, Joe 132
smoke tree 159
smokers 143-4
snowdrop 139, 162
solanum 101, 197-8
sound 8, 31, 50
spiraea 116
Stanstead Park 29
Staw, J.A., and Swander M.: *Parsnips in the Snow* 120
Stone House Cottage Garden 9
straight lines 45-6
structures 47, 53

succulents 157-8
summer 70-4
sunlight 80
sunken garden 45, 97
surrealist garden 29-32, 50
surroundings 28, 34, 53, 66
sweet pepper bush 201
Swift, Katherine 132, 190-1
swimming pools 169-70

tidying 19, 208-9
Tolstoy, Leo: *Anna Karenina* 70
tree platform 68, 86
trees 48, 52, 85, 154-5, 184-5
  training 103-8, 113, 116
trellis work 47, 52, 54
Trifolium repens 153
trompe-l'oeil 52-3, 127-8, 148
Tropaeolum speciosum 159
tropical plants 80-1
tulips 8, 112

urns 123-4, 132-3

variegated plants 164
vegetables 118-21
Verey, Rosemary 191-2
Vésian, Nicole de 25, 46
visiting gardens 6-23, 40, 92-3

walls 48-9, 52, 70, 95, 100
water 50-1, 67, 77, 95, 100-1
water-lily 151
watering 38, 121
weather 34, 43, 76-83
Wheeler, David 190
Whichford Pottery 124
wild flowers 27, 74-5, 205
wild life 66-8
willow 26, 107-8
winter 209-10
wisteria 113
wood 47
writing 188-92

Yates, C.: *The Secret Carp* 67
yew 10, 49, 101-2, 107

zinnia 153, 160